CAREERS IN THE ARMED SERVICES

THE KOGAN PAGE GUIDE TO

CAREERS IN THE ARMED SERVICES

Alan S Watts

KOGAN PAGE

First published in Great Britain in 1989 by Kogan Page Limited, 120 Pentonville Road, London N1 9JN.

British Library Cataloguing in Publication Data
Watts, Alan S.
　The Kogan Page guide to careers in the armed services.
　1.　British military forces
　I.　Title
　355'.00941

　ISBN 1–85091–930–5

Printed and bound in Great Britain by Biddles Limited, Guildford.

Contents

Chapter 1
Introduction

By enlisting in one of the Armed Services, a young man or young woman embarks not so much on a new career as on a new way of life, a life which demands loyalty and exacts discipline and obedience. It also involves being part of a community which shares a corporate pride both in its past and present achievements, and is a close-knit caring community, looking after its members and their dependants.

In this new way of life, there are unsurpassable opportunities to make new friends, acquire new skills, participate in all manner of sports and activities, and broaden your knowledge of the wider world. Finally, it is a way of life which affords real satisfaction, because in the Services, whatever your particular duty might be, every job is a worthwhile job.

The Armed Forces of Great Britain may not be as large as those of the super powers, but they are as well equipped and well trained as any. They work as a team: the capability of one depends, in the last analysis, on the capabilities of the others. They are therefore all under the eventual control of the Secretary of State for Defence, operating through the Chief of the Defence Staff and the chiefs of staff of each service.

The prime role of the Armed Forces is one of defence and in view of this, a large part of the Army and much of the Royal Air Force is stationed in West Germany as Britain's contribution to the North Atlantic Treaty Organisation (NATO). Other Army units and RAF squadrons are based in the UK, while the Royal Navy protects our coasts and sea-lanes.

The Armed Forces have a number of other roles, the chief of which is fulfilled by the Navy's nuclear-powered submarines which lie constantly in readiness in the ocean depths, and offer the threat of instant retaliation to any would-be nuclear aggressor. This role is shared by the bombers of the RAF.

Another important function, fulfilled mainly by the Army, is that of combating terrorism in Northern Ireland and safeguarding lives and property by supporting the Royal Ulster Constabulary.

Berlin, Belize, Hong Kong, the Falkland Islands and Gibraltar are other places where the Forces still maintain a presence.

From time to time there are also calls by the United Nations for assistance in providing peace-keeping forces in various parts of the globe. In addition, there are many duties at home. The Army provides ceremonial guards at the royal palaces and Horse Guards; the Navy's helicopters are constantly called upon for coastal rescue work; the RAF aerobatic display team is to be seen at many air pageants every summer. Overseas, the Navy has maintained a patrol in the Persian Gulf to give protection to British shipping there. It sends its survey vessels to distant parts to survey and chart coastlines and seabeds. And from time to time, it makes courtesy calls to foreign ports, to 'show the flag'.

Every Service needs people of the highest quality – not necessarily those with the highest educational qualifications, though it needs many of these – but people who are fit, intelligent, capable of learning, and with a sound basic education as a grounding for further training.

There are so many trades and occupations within each Service – from telephonists, typists, clerks, cooks and musicians to mechanics, pilots, police, pharmacists and photographers – that there is a place for every type of entrant. The quality of training in the Services is second to none, and it is quite possible to obtain high qualifications, eg BTEC certificates, ONC etc, so that on completion of your service there is little difficulty in obtaining civilian employment.

The Services can also further your general education, and their skilled instructors can help you develop your abilities in various sports and hobbies. All the Services place a great emphasis on sport, and servicemen and women are encouraged to take part in team games, athletics, swimming, mountaineering, and other outdoor activities.

Each Service has its own women's branch. The Women's Royal Naval Service and the Women's Royal Army Corps, although they work closely with the Royal Navy and the Army respectively, are organised as separate bodies. The Women's Royal Air Force, however, is much more integrated. With the exception of RAF apprenticeships, the RAF Regiment, RAF chaplains, pilots and navigators, all RAF careers are equally open to women. Women officers are commissioned into the RAF, and all ranks share duties with their male counterparts.

There is, of course, considerable integration in the WRNS and WRAC, as will be seen from the chapters on the Navy and Army where details of the work in various trades within the women's services are given. These chapters also contain sections dealing especially with these women's services.

It must be emphasised that all the Services are keen to recruit members of ethnic communities, and many of the recruits have served for long periods and reached positions of responsibility.

This guide has relied heavily on the booklets and information provided by the Services, but more detailed information can be obtained from the staff at any of the Careers Information Offices which have been set up throughout the country by each of the three Services. The following pages set out broad details of the requirements of each of the Services, including the Royal Marines, the women's services, and the nursing services. (Note that a high standard of physical fitness and vision is generally required for the various trades.)

Educational Requirements

Educational requirements vary with the trade or rank for which the applicant is applying. Many trades require applicants to have GCSEs or O levels, and in some cases A levels, and essential subjects may be specified. Direct entry to several branches is restricted to qualified persons. However, there are many openings in all three Services for people with no academic qualifications whatsoever, provided they can pass a straightforward test in numeracy and use of the English language.

Nationality

An applicant is not normally eligible unless:

(a) at all times since birth he or she has been either a Commonwealth citizen or a citizen of the Irish Republic, and

(b) he or she was born in a country or territory which is (or then was) within the Commonwealth, or in the Irish Republic, and

(c) each of his or her parents was born in a country or territory which is (or then was) within the Commonwealth, or in the

Irish Republic, and is or was at death a Commonwealth citizen or a citizen of the Irish Republic, and has or had been one or other at all times since birth.

In certain circumstances, these conditions may be relaxed. Advice in this connection may be obtained from the Ministry of Defence (DAR).

Residence

Applicants, whether or not they are of UK origin, should have resided in the UK for a minimum of five years, preferably immediately preceding their application. In certain circumstances, particularly when an applicant is of UK origin, a shorter period of residence may be accepted and part of the residence requirement waived, provided that evidence of assimilation into the UK can be demonstrated.

Advice on this matter may be obtained from the Ministry of Defence (DAR).

Chapter 2
The Royal Navy and Royal Marines

Although the Royal Navy (the Senior Service) has been progressively reduced in size since 1945, it is still one of the most powerful fighting services afloat. Its members are superbly trained, it is equipped with the latest in sophisticated instruments and weaponry, and is entrusted with Britain's main nuclear deterrents. It therefore offers excellent career opportunities to young people (both men and women) of the right calibre who are prepared to work with others as members of a disciplined team, to learn new skills and to work hard, sometimes under very difficult conditions. Life in the Navy and in the Marines can be tough and demanding, but it is also rewarding and satisfying, affording its members many opportunities to gain valuable experience and to exercise responsibility.

Organisation of the Navy

The Royal Navy is divided into eight teams or branches, each containing a number of different trades. Every recruit for the Navy is placed in the available trade for which he or she is most suited and will follow thereafter. Some branches – the *Submarine Branch*, the *Regulating Branch* (which provides the Navy's police), and the *Physical Training Branch* – select their personnel from within the Navy, and therefore are not open to recruits coming direct from civilian life.

The other branches are as follows:

1. *The Operations Branch* is a very large branch and consists of the men who actually 'work the ship' – in other words, they are responsible for getting it in and out of harbour, for anchoring and refuelling. They are also responsible for 'fighting the ship' – that is, for operating the ship's weapon systems. The Operations Branch is divided into two, and the men who do these jobs are all members of the *Seaman Group*.

The *Communications Group* maintains and operates the communications system of the ship, keeping in touch with other ships and aircraft, and with shore stations. It employs a full range of frequencies and equipment, which includes the use of satellites.

2. *The Engineering Branch* has the task of keeping the Navy's ships and aircraft fully operational and ready to put to sea at very short notice. Skilled engineers are needed to look after ships' propulsion systems, electrical generators and switchgear. Others service and maintain the Navy's aircraft and helicopters, while others still are responsible for the Navy's weapons and weapon-support systems. The branch is therefore divided into three groups: *Marine Engineering*, *Air Engineering* and *Weapon Engineering*.

3. *The Supply and Secretariat Branch* looks after the pay, accounting and administrative work of the Navy. It has to ensure that supplies of every conceivable type are readily available – spare parts for weapon

RANKS

Royal Navy	WRNS
Admiral of the Fleet	
Admiral	
Vice Admiral	
Rear Admiral	
Commodore	
Captain	Director WRNS
Commander	Superintendent
Lieutenant Commander	Chief Officer
Lieutenant	First Officer
Sub-Lieutenant	Second Officer
Midshipman	Third Officer
Fleet Chief Petty Officer	Fleet Chief Wren
Chief Petty Officer	Chief Wren
Petty Officer	Petty Officer Wren
Leading Rating	Leading Wren
Able Rating	(Able) Wren
Ordinary Rating	(Ordinary) Wren

systems, blankets, flags, crockery, ball-point pens, and so on. It also keeps records of its stocks so that information is always at hand as to what supplies are available and what needs to be ordered. This branch is also responsible for feeding the Navy's personnel, ie ordering, cooking and serving food.

4. *The Medical Branch* employs doctors, dentists, physiotherapists, radiographers, and various types of medical assistant.

5. *The Fleet Air Arm* flies and maintains the variety of aircraft used by the Navy on ships and naval air stations.

Naval Ratings

Age Requirements
For most Navy jobs, applicants should be aged between 16 and 33, but for some categories they should be older than 16, and the upper age limit is lower (see details of specific requirements for jobs, given below). Entrants under the age of 17½ join as juniors, others as Ordinary Ratings.

Education
No special educational requirements are needed for most Navy jobs. New entrants take a short selection test to ensure they are literate, numerate and can do simple mechanical problems. (See details of specific jobs for particular educational requirements.)

How to Apply
There are Royal Navy and Royal Marines Careers Information Offices throughout the country (you will find their addresses at the end of this chapter, and in the telephone book under 'Naval Establishments'). You can telephone or write to the office, but it is better to make a personal visit so that you can discuss your particular circumstances with the naval personnel, who will advise you on the current situation. They will also help you with the next stage of joining the Navy on your second visit – after you have had a chance to read through the booklets you have been given and consider whether you are really serious about enlisting. If you are, you will be interviewed, medically examined and put through the selection test.

Basic Training

All ratings do their basic training at HMS *Raleigh*, the Navy's New Entry Training Establishment in Cornwall. Seamen Operators, Survey Recorders, and certain other categories remain at HMS *Raleigh* for further training and subsequently sub-specialise at other establishments. Other categories do their further training at appropriate specialist training establishments.

Choice of Trade

The following categories can be entered between the ages of 16 and 33, and except where stated, no special educational requirements are demanded:

Operations Branch

Seaman Group

Radar Operator. Works in the Operations Room, plotting the position of ships and aircraft on radar.

Sonar Operator. Operates sonar (listening) equipment to hunt surface ships and submarines.

Electronic Warfare Operator. Listens in on friendly and hostile communications and signals.

Missile Operator. Looks after the control and operation of the ship's missiles.

Mine Warfare Operator. Works in special ships looking for and disposing of mines.

Survey Recorder. Helps to make charts of coastlines and seabeds. Works in special computer-assisted ships all over the world.

Communications Group

Radio Operator (General). Handles day-to-day signal traffic and provides radio equipment for other departments of the ship.

Radio Operator (Tactical). Uses radio equipment in the tactical movement of ships.

Radio Operator (Submarines). Has expertise in the special communications systems used in submarines.

Engineering Branch

Marine Engineering Mechanic. May specialise in either *Mechanical* engineering, working on engines and propulsion systems, or *Electrical* engineering, dealing with the various kinds of generators, electrical switchgear, and large electrical equipment.

Weapon Engineering Mechanic. May also specialise, dealing with *Ordnance*, helping to service the weapons systems, or with *Radio*, on high-tech maritime radio, radar, sonar, and navigation equipment.

Air Engineering Mechanic. Services and repairs aircraft; works on airframes and radio equipment. May choose one of three specialisms – *Mechanical, Radio,* or *Weapon Electrical*.

Fleet Air Arm Branch

Naval Airman (Aircraft Handling). Ensures that aircraft take off and land safely and are secured after landing. Also specialises in fire-fighting. Some aircraft handlers, when qualified as *Leading Rates,* are selected to specialise as *Photographers*.

Naval Airman (Survival Equipment). Ensures that all life-saving equipment (parachutes, lifejackets, life-rafts, protective clothing and radio devices) on an aircraft is in working order.

Naval Airman (Meteorology). Records weather information. Applicants for Naval Airman (Met) must have acceptable GCSE/O-level passes (or equivalent) in mathematics or a science subject or meteorology or geography.

Medical Branch

Medical Technicians. Must be over 17. Training is given in the following specialisms to applicants with the necessary qualifications:

Physiotherapist. Requires five acceptable GCSE/GCE passes or equivalent, to include English and certain science subjects. Two passes at A level or equivalent are required.

Radiographer. Requires seven acceptable GCSE/GCE passes with two at A level or equivalent. English and mathematics or physics are compulsory. An acceptable alternative is ONC or OND in a science subject.

Laboratory Technician. Requires five acceptable GCSE/O level passes or equivalent. These must include English, mathematics, chemistry, or other science subject.

Pharmacy Dispenser. Requires five acceptable GCSE/O level passes or equivalent, to include English, mathematics, and two science subjects.

Naval Health Inspector. Requires two A levels and five acceptable GCSEs/O levels or equivalent. These must include English, mathematics, and two science subjects.

It should be noted that direct entry as medical technician may also be available to those who already hold the appropriate qualifications.

Medical Assistant. Must be over 17. Works with health team. No special educational qualifications required.

Supply and Secretariat Branch
Writer. Carries out a wide range of clerical and administrative duties, in ships and shore establishments.
Stores Accountant. Keeps records of stores, uses computer to check levels of stock, etc.
Cook. Prepares and serves meals in ships and shore establishments.
Steward. Looks after accommodation and running of the wardroom (the officers' mess).

Artificers

Artificers are the most skilled engineering technicians in the Navy. They fall into three main categories:

Air Engineering Artificer, with specialisation in either Weapons, Electrical, Radio, or Mechanical.
Marine Engineering Artificer, with specialisation in either Mechanical or Electrical, and
Weapon Engineering Artificer, with specialisations in Action Data; Communications and Electronic Warfare; Weapon Data and Ordnance Control.

Apprenticeship and Direct Entry
Entry as Artificer Apprentice is between the ages of 16 and 21 on the first day of the month of entry. Applicants must pass a selection test, aptitude tests, interview, medical examination, and qualify in a special written examination. A candidate may obtain exemption from the examination by:

(a) gaining acceptable grades at GCSE/O level in physics or a suitable physics-based science subject, mathematics, and English or an acceptable alternative;

(b) satisfactorily completing the first year of an appropriate BTEC Certificate or Diploma programme in Engineering with passes in six Units at Level I, including pass-with-merit in mathematics and engineering science, together with an acceptable grade at GCSE/O level in English or an acceptable alternative;

(c) producing evidence of having passed any other examination acceptable to the Ministry of Defence (Navy Department).

Training lasts five years. On completion of five years' service and on suitable recommendation, apprentices are advanced to Petty Officer.

Direct entry as Artificer in the same categories is available under certain circumstances to candidates aged between 19½ and 33. They should hold a suitable BTEC Diploma or ONC in engineering with passes in mathematics and two other acceptable subjects; or a City and Guilds Technician Certificate (Part II) or equivalent qualifications. They should have completed an acceptable engineering apprenticeship and be an appropriately qualified technician or technician engineer.

Direct entry Artificers receive approximately 21 to 25 months' naval engineering training. They enter as Probationary Leading Artificers. On completion of Part 1 training and subject to recommendation, those aged 22 and over are advanced to Acting Petty Officer Artificer (after approximately six weeks). Petty Officer rate is usually achieved after about six months.

Terms of Engagement

Royal Navy and Royal Marines recruits are entered for 22 years' service from the age of 18 or date of entry if later. This service is pensionable. There is no requirement to re-engage at the end of this time, but there are opportunities for selected ratings to sign on for an additional five years in order to complete 27 years' service, and possibly for a further five years to complete 32 years, so earning a considerably higher pension and terminal grant.

Breaking the Engagement

All ratings have the right to claim discharge on giving 18 months' notice at any time after completing two years six months' service after the age of 18. A minimum of four years' trained service must be completed.

During service there are opportunities to take higher training courses, but ratings will not be allowed to take certain of these unless they waive the right to give notice as outlined above for an agreed period.

Premature release

Those who for one reason or another decide soon after joining that they are not suited for the Service can apply to leave as follows:

(a) Under 18 on joining: during the first six months of service or before reaching the age of 18 years 3 months, whichever is the earlier.

(b) Aged 18 and over on joining: during the first three months of service.

Those under the age of 17½ on entry must give 14 days' notice of intention to leave. Those over 17½ on entry must pay a sum up to the equivalent of seven days' gross pay.

Royal Fleet Reserve Liability
Ratings leaving before completion of their full engagement, other than those taking premature release, have a liability for up to three years' service in the Royal Fleet Reserve.

Pay
The following table shows the monthly basic pay (as at 1 April 1989) for the rates at which it is possible to join the Service:

Junior under age of 16½ (RM also)	£277
Junior from age of 16½ (RM also)	£309
Junior from age of 17 (RM also)	£375
Ordinary Seaman (aged 17½ and over) and Marine 2nd Class	£496–£563
Artificer Apprentices and Communications and Medical Technicians (during first year of training)	£366

Naval Officers

Types of Commission
There are two main types of commission – full career and short career (although reference is sometimes made to medium career commissions). Most naval officers enter on a full career commission. They are assured, subject to certain conditions, of a career to the age of 50 or beyond according to rank. Full career commissions are offered in the Seaman, Supply and Secretariat, and Engineering specialisations.

Short career commissions vary in length from 5 to 16 years, depending on the specialisation and the wishes of the officer. Because of this range in the length of short careers, they are often divided into short and medium career commissions. At the conclusion of a short career commission, an officer receives a tax-free gratuity, while officers concluding a medium career commission qualify for an Armed Forces pension.

Short career commissions are available in the Seaman, Supply and Secretariat, Engineering, and Flying Duties specialisations. Seaman, and Supply and Secretariat officers are offered an eight-year commission with the option of leaving after five years – in either case receiving a gratuity. Engineer officers are offered a 16-year commission or service until the age of 38 (whichever is the later) at the end of which service they qualify for an Armed Forces pension. Aircrew officers are offered a similar 16-year commission, or a 12-year commission with a break after eight years. Instructor officers are offered a five- or eight-year commission with the option to leave after three or five years. A gratuity is paid for each year's service on retirement after three, five, or eight years. Medical and dental officers are offered a five-year commission, with a gratuity on leaving the Service after five years. After two years' service there is the opportunity to apply for a transfer to a pensionable commission.

Full Career Commissions

Methods of Entry
Selection for all entries is by interview and medical examination. For the Seaman Branch and Flying Duties, a high standard of eyesight, including colour perception, is required, but a lower standard may be accepted for other branches.

The selection panel usually consists of two or three naval officers, a civilian headmaster, and a personnel selection officer. The selection process includes a variety of tests which take place over two and a half days at HMS *Sultan*, a naval shore establishment at Gosport (details of the tests and interviews are sent to candidates in advance).

The first day involves a series of written aptitude tests designed to discover the extent of the candidate's general and naval knowledge, plus a short essay on a general topic. The second day begins with initiative tests, when candidates take it in turns to lead a group across a series of obstacles. This is followed by a planning and discussion exercise, when candidates are asked to provide a solution to an imaginary emergency situation. Finally, there is an interview with the Admiralty Interview Board.

Sponsorships
There are three types of sponsorship scheme available to young

people: university cadetships, bursaries, and scholarship entry. All candidates have to attend the Admiralty Interview Board (for further details, see below).

1. University Cadetship Scheme This scheme is also applicable to RM and WRNS candidates. University Cadetships enable a candidate to take a degree and also obtain a full career commission in either the Seaman, Supply and Secretariat, or Engineering specialisations. Candidates must be aged 17 and under 22 on the first day of the month of entry. Candidates for the Seaman or Supply and Secretariat specialisation must have a place or a definite offer of a place at a British university or polytechnic, leading to a recognised UK degree. They must have five GCSE/GCE or SCE passes, to include English and mathematics. Of the five passes, either two must be at A level or three SCE at Higher Grade.

Candidates for the Engineering specialisation must have a place leading to a degree in mechanical, electrical, electronic, or aeronautical engineering or a closely related engineering subject. They must have five GCSE/GCE or SCE passes including English, and mathematics and physics at A level or Higher Grade. University cadets are paid as officers while at university or polytechnic.

2. Bursaries This scheme is also applicable to RM and WRNS candidates. Holders of a bursary remain civilians during their time at university or polytechnic. They undertake a minimum return of three years' service after their studies and naval professional training are over, but they are free to choose either a full or short or medium career commission. They receive an annual tax-free bursary in addition to the LEA grant. Requirements are similar to those for university cadetships.

3. Scholarships and Reserved Places Scheme (not available for WRNS candidates) The Ministry of Defence offers a number of scholarships each year to assist boys to obtain the necessary A levels or H Grades for naval college entry. The parents or guardians of scholarship-holders are assisted financially during the last two years of their sons' schooling. Candidates who, although failing to gain a scholarship, are highly recommended in the selection process may be awarded reserved places at the naval college. The scheme is limited to intending Royal Marines officers and Royal Navy officers in the Seaman and Engineering specialisations.

Candidates for Royal Marines and Royal Navy (Seaman) commissions require five GCSE or O-level passes or five SCE Ordinary Grades, including English and mathematics. There must be no break in education between GCSE/O levels (or SCE O Grades) and A levels (or Highers).

Candidates for Royal Navy (Engineering) commissions require similar passes except that their GCSEs or equivalent must include a physics-based science.

Naval College Entry
Applicants should be aged 17 and under 23 on the first day of the month of entry. Those wishing to become Seaman or Supply and Secretariat officers require five GCSE/GCE or SCE passes, including English and mathematics. Of the five passes, two must be at A level or 3 SCE at Higher Grade. Candidates wishing to become Engineer officers require 5 GCSE/O-level or SCE passes including English, and mathematics and physics at A level or Higher Grade.

Direct Graduate Entry
This method of entry is for young men under the age of 26 who do not decide on a naval career until graduating or approaching the end of their degree courses. Those applying for Seaman or Supply and Secretariat full career commissions should possess a UK degree and GCSE/O-level or SCE passes in English and mathematics. Intending Engineer officers should have a degree in mechanical, electrical, electronic, or aeronautical engineering or a closely related subject acceptable to the Ministry of Defence. Candidates should also possess a GCSE/O-level or O-grade pass in English.

Short Career Commissions

Naval College Entry
Candidates should be aged 17 and under 26 on the first day of the month of entry. Candidates for Seaman and Supply and Secretariat specialisations and for Flying Duties require five GCSE/O-level or SCE passes, including English and mathematics. Candidates for the Engineering specialisation require either

Five GCSE/O-level or SCE passes including English, and mathematics and physics at A level or Higher Grade;
GCSE/O-level or SCE Ordinary Grade passes in English and one other subject, and BTEC Certificate or Diploma passes with merit at Level III in mathematics and two units of engineering principles.

Direct Graduate Entry

Candidates should be under the age of 26 on the first day of the month of entry. Candidates for Seaman and Supply and Secretariat specialities and for flying duties require a UK degree and GCSE/O-level or SCE passes in English and mathematics. Candidates for Engineering specialisations must have GCSE/O-level or SCE passes in English. They must also possess a UK degree in mechanical, electrical, electronic or aeronautical engineering, or an alternative recognised qualification.

There are facilities for mature applicants between the ages of 26 and 32 to obtain short career commissions in the Engineering specialisation. They must have the appropriate qualifications and satisfy the Ministry of Defence of continuance of employment in the engineering field and provide evidence of acceptable professional experience.

Instructors

Applicants for short career commissions as Instructor should be under the age of 34, and hold a UK degree or equivalent, or a professional qualification (HND or HNC in engineering), or teaching qualifications acceptable to the Ministry of Defence, and GCSE/O-level of SCE passes in English, mathematics, and a physics-based science. The main requirement is for men with qualifications in engineering, physics or mathematics.

Medical and Dental Officers

There are opportunities for medical and dental cadetships. Medical and dental cadets should preferably be under 25 on attaining the second MB/BDS or equivalent. Applications may be made six months before the examination.

Other medical entry includes

Pre-registration Entry, for which applicants, preferably under 33, must be in pre-registration year;

Qualified and Registered Entry, for which medical applicants must be under 39, and dental applicants under 32. Candidates must be qualified practitioners or dental surgeons.

Naval Chaplains

Candidates should be under the age of 35 and physically fit. They must be recommended by their respective church authorities, must be ordained, and normally have had two or more years' experience of parish work.

Officer Duties

1. Seaman Officers have the responsibility of 'working' and 'fighting' the ship. As Bridge Watchkeeping officers they are responsible to the commanding officer for the safe and efficient handling of the vessel throughout a four-hour watch period. They must not only be first-class seamen, but also understand fully their ships' capabilities and limitations as fighting vessels. Only Seaman Officers can aspire to the command of a naval vessel at sea.

After their initial training at the Britannia Royal Naval College, Seaman Officers complete their general training with up to 12 months' practical experience at sea, when they might serve on any type of naval vessel – minehunter, frigate, anti-submarine carrier, etc. This prepares them for the Fleet Board examination. Having passed the examination, they move on to further professional training, such as the 16-week Officer of the Watch Course. Full career officers might also take the Principal Warfare Officer Course.

There are several areas in which Seaman Officers may sub-specialise:

Aircraft Control. Naval aircraft controllers are responsible for the guidance and tactical control of fighter and attack fixed-wing aircraft, helicopters, and maritime reconnaissance aircraft, using radar and computer systems. This sub-specialisation follows a five-month training course, open to both full and short career officers.

Aviation. Officers may train as observers or pilots, flying naval helicopters. A small number are selected to fly Sea Harriers ('jump jets'). Aircrew officers also take part in amphibious warfare, search and rescue operations, casualty evacuation, communication work and reconnaissance. Aircrew start training before they reach the age of 27.

Mine Warfare and Clearance Diving (MCD). A four-week course is taken to qualify as a ship's diving officer. Successful officers may be nominated for a seven-month MCD course, in which they learn to dive to 180 feet. They also learn the techniques for locating and disposing of mines on the seabed. This sub-specialisation is open to both full and short career officers.

Submarines. Submariners attend an initial training course at HMS *Dolphin*, at Gosport, followed by a year's sea training in a nuclear-powered Fleet submarine or a diesel-electric Patrol submarine. The Navy also has four nuclear-powered Polaris submarines, each carrying 16 nuclear missiles. Polaris and Fleet submarines can circumnavigate the globe without surfacing. This sub-specialisation is open to full and short career officers. The preferred starting age is under 23½.

Hydrographic Surveying. This small but important sub-specialisation is open to both full and short career officers who, once trained, remain in this sub-specialisation throughout their careers. Initial training is a three-month course at HMS *Drake* at Devonport, before appointment to either an ocean or coastal survey ship. The work consists of hydrographic and oceanographic surveying to provide information for charts used by the Royal Navy and ships of many other countries.

Seaman officers of whatever sub-specialisation perform several duties in the course of their employment. They act as divisional officers responsible for a number of ratings, getting to know them all individually and looking after their welfare and progress. After several years' service they may take the Principal Warfare Officer course.

2. Supply and Secretariat officers deal with the administration necessary to feed, clothe, equip and pay the personnel aboard ship or in shore establishments. The duties may be grouped into four:

Captain's Secretary handles the official correspondence as well as administrative, welfare and personnel matters on a ship or shore establishment. This may involve giving legal advice, so the Supply Officer Course includes training in naval law.

Naval Stores. The stores department of a warship may carry a range of 40,000 items to provide spares for all the equipment on board.

Catering. Supply officers are in charge of the long-term ordering of food and provisions, and for the day-to-day supervision of meals served both in the wardroom and the ratings' messes.

Pay and Cash involves handling the pay of officers and ratings. In a large shore establishment this can add up to several million pounds each year. Duties also include the payment of allowances, dealings in foreign exchange, and the keeping of accounts.

Over and above these responsibilities, which might all fall to one officer, Supply and Secretariat officers also have operational duties to perform at sea. These could be in the operations room, the nerve centre of the ship's weapons systems, or as Flight Deck Officer, helping to ensure the safe take-off and landing of the ship's helicopters, or playing a major part in the damage control organisation.

Supply officers also act as divisional officers in charge of 20 or more ratings. A Supply officer might also act as the ship's adventure training officer, taking the men canoeing, hiking on Dartmoor, or skiing. Some Supply officers have even qualified to become their ship's diving officer.

3. Engineer officers perform such a wide range of functions that their work is divided into five sub-specialisations:

Weapon Engineer Officer (Surface Ships). Responsible for all the ship's weapon systems, including all aspects of the weapons' sensors and communications systems such as sonars, radars, computer systems, satellite communications, and all gun, torpedo, and missile systems.

Weapon Engineer Officer (Submarines). A similar responsibility to that of WEO (Surface Ships) but with the additional duty of being control room watchkeeper. The WEO on Polaris submarines is responsible for all aspects of the missiles.

Marine Engineer Officer (Surface Ships). Responsible for the ship's hull and general structures; main engines and all auxiliary machinery; the main electrical generators and the electrical distribution system; the air conditioning, ventilating, and heating systems; the cold rooms, and all fuel and water systems.

Marine Engineer Officer (Submarines). Similar responsibility as MEO (Surface Ships) but also concerned with nuclear reactors and specialised submarine hull equipment.

Air Engineer Officer (Mechanical and Electrical). Responsible for keeping naval aircraft fully operational and ensuring the safety of aircrew. Deals with maintenance and defect-repair of all aircraft systems, including airframe, engine, weapon and control systems. May be given the opportunity to train as test pilot.

Basic Pay for RN and RM Officers (as at 1 April 1989)
The following basic rates apply to the ranks at which it is possible to join the Service. In some of these cases, certain officers may receive extra pay according to seniority credits (for fuller details see form CP22).

Midshipman on entry	£6,782 per annum
University cadetship entry	£6,001 in first year, made up of part-pay and an element for education grant. In addition, tuition fees are paid by the Ministry of Defence.
(RN) Midshipman: Sub-Lieutenant	
(RM) 2nd Lieutenant: Acting Lieutenant	
2nd Lieutenant RM on appointment	£8,428 per annum
Graduate, on entry as Sub-Lieutenant	£9,662 per annum

Charges and Allowances
The following charges currently apply to RN and RM officers:

Food. There is a continuous monthly charge of £79.08 for single officers accommodated in shore establishments at home and abroad. However, there is no charge for officers when serving afloat.
Accommodation. Single officers living in pay a monthly charge for standard accommodation ashore. This varies from £45.00 to £117.18. However, midshipmen when entering the service and recruits on the university cadetship entry scheme at Dartmouth pay only £16.50 per month.
Married Quarters. The charges for married couples living in the Service's married quarters vary, depending on type of accommodation, etc.

Officers are entitled to claim the following allowances:

Removal Expenses. When a new appointment involves moving house, the Navy will pay all removal expenses, as well as fares for the family, and a disturbance allowance.
Bursaries. For each year at university RN, RM and WRNS officers receive a bursary for the sum of £1,200.

Women's Royal Naval Service

Although members of the WRNS (Wrens) do not serve at sea in HM ships, some have an opportunity to go overseas. They may find themselves working in NATO Headquarters in Europe, or with naval detachments in Gibraltar, Hong Kong, or the Falkland Islands. The majority, however, are stationed in the United Kingdom: some in London; others in naval establishments, such as those at Portsmouth and Plymouth; or at training depots, such as the Britannia Royal Naval College at Dartmouth; or at naval air stations, such as HMS *Gannet* in Scotland; or Royal Marines establishments, such as that at Deal.

Ratings

Girls wishing to enter the WRNS as ratings should apply to their nearest Royal Navy Careers Information Office. Here they can talk to experienced members of the WRNS who will answer questions about the Service. They will also learn what jobs are currently available and for which they might be qualified. Recruits should be aged 17 and will be accepted up to and including the day of their 28th birthday. Girls may apply to join at any time after the age of 16¾, but those under the age of 18 need the consent of their parents or guardian. Before being accepted, they must pass a selection test, an interview and medical examination. If these are satisfactory, they then proceed to HMS *Raleigh* near Plymouth for five weeks' basic training.

During these five weeks, the recruits are introduced to naval customs and organisation. They learn about the various ranks in the Navy and how to distinguish them. They are given parade-ground training and practise fire-fighting, sailing, first-aid, self-defence, and map-reading. On the third weekend of training they make an expedition to Dartmoor where they spend a couple of days camping out, in all weathers. They have to cook their own rations, and use their map-reading skills to find their way to a final rendez-vous.

Jobs

Once Wrens have completed their basic training, they will find a variety of job opportunities, some of which do not require any special educational qualifications. For example:

Wren Telephonist. Operates a variety of switchboards and is trained to deal with emergencies. Must be prepared to work shifts, both day and night. Specialist training: four weeks at HMS *Seahawk*, Culdrose, Cornwall.

Wren Writer. Engaged in general clerical and secretarial duties –

typing, answering correspondence, duplicating, filing, operating word-processor and maintaining records. Specialist training: 13 weeks at HMS *Raleigh*, Torpoint, Cornwall.

Wren Stores Accountant. Responsible for ordering, storing, issuing and accounting for items required to support ships and aircraft, shore establishments and personnel. Specialist training: nine weeks at HMS *Raleigh*, Torpoint, Cornwall. Wren Stores Accountants have the opportunity to take further courses leading to Royal Society of Arts examinations.

Wren Steward. Helps to ensure the smooth running of the officers' mess. Undertakes a variety of domestic responsibilities such as making beds, cleaning rooms, caring for officers' uniforms, waiting at table, serving behind the bar, etc. Shares with naval ratings the ceremonial duties at guest-night dinners in naval wardrooms. Specialist training: six weeks at HMS *Raleigh*, Torpoint, Cornwall. Wren Stewards have the opportunity to take further courses leading to City and Guilds examinations.

Wren Dental Surgery Assistant. Assists the dental surgeon in the treatment of patients of all ranks. Keeps appointment and record books and may be involved with minor clerical and storekeeping tasks. Specialist training: 12 weeks at HMS *Nelson*, Portsmouth.

Wren Air Engineering Mechanic. Services and repairs the systems and equipment of naval aircraft. A minimum height of 5ft 1 inch is required for this work. Mechanics specialise in one of three engineering trades – Mechanical, Radio, or Weapons Electrical. Specialist training: 16 weeks (Mechanical), 22 weeks (Radio), and 25 weeks (Weapons Electrical). Training for all trades is at the Air Engineering School, HMS *Daedalus*, Lee-on-Solent, Hants, followed by a period of practical consolidation training at a naval air station. There are opportunities for some Wren Air Engineering Mechanics to be selected for training as Air Engineering Technicians (Artificer).

Wren Radar. Interprets the information appearing on radar screens in order to plot positions on maps and charts, and to evaluate the results of exercises, often with the help of computers. Specialist training: six weeks at HMS *Dryad*, near Portsmouth.

Wren Radio Operator. Responsible for relaying signals from large communications centres to ships and shore bases throughout the world, or re-routing and distributing incoming signals. In the main signal office, operators despatch messages by teleprinter and type messages for internal distribution. Specialist training: nine weeks at HMS *Mercury*, Petersfield, Hants.

Entrants to other trades require particular educational qualifications. For example:

Wren Weapon Analyst. Responsible for analysing the results of weapon practices, sometimes using computers. Also responsible for assessing films and written records of ship, submarine and aircraft weapon firings. Weapon analysts work flexible hours, and occasionally have the opportunity to go to sea for a few days during exercises. Specialist training: nine weeks at HMS *Dryad*, near Portsmouth. Educational requirement:

☐ GCSE/GCE O level or equivalent in specified subjects.

Wren Meteorological Observer. Collects weather data, such as rainfall and temperature, wind speed and direction, and prepares weather charts from data obtained by instruments, teleprinter messages from weather stations, etc. The work may include oceanography. Specialist training: nine weeks at HMS *Seahawk*, Culdrose, Cornwall. Educational requirement:

☐ GCSE/GCE O level or equivalent in specified subjects.

Wren Education and Training Support. Looks after libraries, information and display rooms, etc. Assists in production of audio and visual aids; has the care and maintenance of audio-visual equipment, such as projectors and closed-circuit TV. In more senior positions, may be called upon to teach mathematics and English to junior naval ratings. Specialist training: three weeks at HMS *Raleigh*, Torpoint, Cornwall, followed by five weeks at the RN School of Education and Training Technology, HMS *Nelson*, Portsmouth. Educational requirement:

☐ GCSE/GCE O level or equivalent in specified subjects.

There are certain jobs for which only Wrens who have been in the Service for some time may apply. These include:

Regulator. Responsible for discipline (the WRNS police). Transfer to Regulator duties brings advancement to Acting Leading Wren on completion of training (minimum height for acceptance: 5ft 4 inches). Specialist training: 11 weeks at HMS *Drake*, Plymouth.

Physical Trainer. Related more to recreational and expeditionary sports than to physical fitness. On completion of training, Wren Physical Trainers are advanced to Acting Leading Wrens. Specialist training: 25 weeks at HMS *Temeraire*, Portsmouth.

Family Services. Looking after the welfare of Service personnel and their families. Specialist training: 12 weeks at HMS *Drake*, Plymouth. Educational requirement:

☐ GCSE/GCE O level or equivalent in specified subjects.

Wren Photographer. Assists in providing a shore-based photographic service for the Royal Navy and Royal Marines. The work covers cine, video and still photography. On completion of training, Wren Photographers are advanced to Acting Leading Wrens. Specialist training: 10 weeks at the Joint School of Photography, RAF Cosford, Wolverhampton. Educational requirement:

☐ GCSE/GCE O level or equivalent in specified subjects.

Basic Pay for WRNS Ratings (as at 1 April 1989)

Ordinary Rating under the age of 17½	£363 per month
Ordinary Rating from the age of 17½	£492 per month

Further details about rates of pay can be found in leaflet CP11, available from the Royal Navy and Royal Marines Careers Information Offices.

WRNS Officers

All WRNS officer candidates applying for direct entry must do so between the ages of 20½ and 26½. They need to have, or be in the process of acquiring, the educational requirements for the specialisation they wish to enter:

Direct Entry (General)
Any UK degree or Certificate of Education and GCSE/O-level passes (or equivalent) in English and mathematics.

Direct Entry (Air Engineering)
Opportunities exist for women with a UK degree in aeronautical engineering and a GCSE/O-level pass (or equivalent) in English.

Direct Entry (Instructor)
A UK degree in mathematics, physics, or engineering, and GCSE/O-level passes (or equivalent) in English and mathematics.

Direct Entry (Secretarial)
One year's full-time secretarial training, followed by at least two years in a responsible post, and five GCSE/O-level passes (or equivalent), including English and mathematics.

Direct Entry (Catering)
An appropriate three-year course leading to a degree or HND, followed by two years' responsible professional experience and five GCSE/O-level passes (or equivalent), including English and mathematics.

Direct Entry (Physical Training)
Recognised full-time training leading to a degree or Qualified Teacher's Certificate in PE; also five GCSE/O-level passes (or equivalent), including English and mathematics.

All entrants are engaged on an eight years' short service commission with the option to leave after five years and the right to apply for a pensionable commission. A gratuity is payable on leaving the Service after five or eight years.

Application Procedure
Applicants should first see a WRNS careers officer or university liaison officer for an advisory interview, following which an application form may be completed. A preliminary interview and aptitude test are arranged, and if at this stage an applicant is short-listed for a commission, she is invited to attend the Admiralty Interview Board (AIB) at HMS *Sultan*, in Gosport. An applicant's suitability is assessed through further intelligence and aptitude tests, a written paper and group discussion with other candidates. This is followed by an interview with the WRNS personnel selection officer, and a second interview with the other members of the board.

Successful candidates who meet the physical and visual standards are invited to the New Entry Training Establishment at Torpoint, Cornwall, for a five-week naval training course. When this is completed, new entrants move on to a naval establishment for a two-month 'acquaint' period, to enable them to get to know about various branches of the Service. They then join the Officers' Training Course at the Britannia Royal Naval College, Dartmouth.

Cadet Entry
Applicants must be aged 18½ and under 25, and have five GCSE/GCE subjects or equivalent (including English and mathematics) with two A-level passes at grade C or above (or 3 SCE at Higher grade). Certain OND/ONC and HND/HNC qualifications will be considered.

Those who wish to be considered should apply at a Royal Navy Careers Information Office for interview, aptitude test and medical examination. Short-listed applicants are then seen by a selection board in London. Selected candidates may normally expect to join the WRNS within six months of attending the selection board (subject to vacancies).

Cadet Wrens undergo both the basic and specialist training of a WRNS rating and are employed as such for the remainder of their first 12 or 15 months' service. Near the end of this time, they attend the selection board for officer candidates (the Admiralty Interview Board at HMS *Sultan*, Gosport) and those who are successful move on to officer training at the Britannia Royal Naval College, Dartmouth.

If at any time between entry to the WRNS and promotion to officer a cadet Wren wishes to withdraw from training, or is considered unsuitable, her service can be terminated. Should she wish to remain in the WRNS, she may apply for enrolment as a WRNS rating with the opportunity of being selected for the Officers' Training Course at a later date.

Rating Entry
WRNS ratings who show officer potential may be selected to attend the Admiralty Interview Board. They must have five GCSEs/O levels (or equivalent), including English and mathematics. If successful at the AIB they will be considered, in competition with other candidates, for the Officers' Training Course. They must be of an age which allows them to be promoted by their 27th birthday.

University Cadetship Scheme
See page 20 in section 'Naval Officers' for details of this entry scheme.

Queen Alexandra's Royal Naval Nursing Service

Queen Alexandra's Royal Naval Nursing Service (QARNNS) is part of the Royal Naval Medical Service; it is therefore fully a part of the Royal Navy and subject to naval discipline like other branches. It has the task of providing a nursing service for the 75,000 people – personnel of the Royal Navy, Royal Marines, and WRNS – who form the naval community, as well as the civilians who live in the area of the Royal Naval hospitals at Gosport, Plymouth, and Gibraltar.

QARNNS has both male and female nurses in its ranks, working in the Royal Naval hospitals, sick bays, and medical centres in a variety of shore establishments. In wartime, nurses may serve in hospital ships. Some served afloat during the Korean War, and, more recently, in SS *Uganda* during the Falklands campaign.

Methods of Entry

Entry into QARNNS has to be restricted because the service is not a large one. There is therefore considerable competition, and only the best applicants are chosen. Also, because places may not be immediately available, applicants are sometimes asked to wait a month or two before taking part in the selection procedure.

There are two categories within QARNNS: a *nursing category* made up of Nursing Officers, student nurses, and direct entry Enrolled Nurses (General) (EN(G)); and a *non-nursing category* known as *Clerical and Quarters*, with officers and assistants. The non-nursing category looks after the management of nurses' quarters and performs clerical and secretarial work within Royal Naval hospitals.

Candidates may apply to join QARNNS from the age of 16½ but cannot begin training until the age of 18, nor beyond the age of 28. They must already have the minimum educational requirements for the particular class of entry, ie:

> *Probationary Student Nurse.* A minimum of five academic GCSE/ O-level passes (or equivalent) obtained at one sitting, of which English is compulsory.
>
> *Clerical and Quarters Assistant* (who may enter between the ages of 18½ and 30) requires a GCSE/O level (or equivalent) in English, or to have passed the RN Educational Test. Typing experience is also essential.
>
> *Qualified Enrolled Nurse (General)* between the ages of 20 and 28 can apply for direct entry.

The first step for candidates for any type of entry is to get in touch with their nearest Royal Navy Careers Information Office. The staff there will advise on how to proceed with the application and answer any questions about such matters as terms of service, conditions, pay, etc. Candidates are invited to take an aptitude test, given a medical examination, and interviewed by serving officers who will decide which candidates satisfy the requirements of QARNNS and can be recommended for acceptance. Female candidates must be at least 4 ft 10 inches tall, and male candidates 5 ft 3 inches, and neither should be more than 25 per cent outside the standard weight for their height and age.

The next step is a professional selection interview at the Royal Naval Hospital, Haslar, Gosport. Candidates are invited to spend the night prior to the interview at the hospital, giving them the opportunity to meet the trainees and qualified nurses already there, and to relax before the interview on the following morning.

The interview is conducted by the Chief Nursing Officer and the Head of Nurse Education. They are anxious to find out what sort of person the applicant is, how highly motivated, how intelligent and adaptable, and whether he or she is likely to be a loyal member of a close-knit team. They endeavour to put the candidate at ease and do their best to make the interview as friendly and straightforward as possible. Candidates cannot expect to hear immediately whether they have been successful, but the results should not be too long. After notification, successful candidates are shortly called to begin their training at HMS *Raleigh*.

Training

All new recruits to QARNNS, whether Probationary Student Nurses, direct entry Enrolled Nurses, or Clerical and Quarters Assistants, receive exactly the same basic training at HMS *Raleigh*. New arrivals are first appointed to a particular 'division' – that is, to one of the groups of trainees making up the New Entry Block. The course is designed to give new entrants a basic knowledge of the Royal Navy, to make them realise they are a part of a large team, and to get them into peak physical condition. They therefore attend lectures on naval practices, customs and traditions; they learn about uniforms, ranks and rates; they practise marching and saluting, and are taught how to fight fires; in the gymnasium they have daily exercises, climb ropes, vault over horses, and so on. Finally, at the end of five strenuous weeks, they attend an impressive passing-out parade, watched by their parents and friends.

Student Nurses

The training period for Student Nurses lasts three years and ten weeks. Probationers who are successful in the School of Nursing examinations held at the end of the first year become Student Nurses.

Nursing training, which takes place at the Royal Naval Hospital, Haslar, follows the syllabus set by the English National Board, and is therefore the same as that for other nurses, both in the Services and outside. Clinical experience is obtained mainly in naval hospitals, and experience in such specialities as psychiatric, obstetric and community nursing, in National Health hospitals. At the end of the training period, Student Nurses sit the final examination leading to registration as Registered General Nurse (RGN).

At this stage, the RGN may stay at Haslar or be transferred to Stonehouse Hospital, Plymouth. At either establishment, the RGN gains further experience while awaiting allocation to some other hospital. When a nurse has been registered for two years, it is possible to apply for a commission as nursing officer.

Clerical and Quarters Assistants

The selection procedure is similar to that for Student Nurses, but the interview at Haslar is conducted by the Chief Nursing Officer and the Clerical and Quarters Officer. Successful candidates undertake five weeks' new entry training at HMS *Raleigh* in the same way as other new entrants. They then spend two weeks at either the Royal Naval Hospital, Haslar, or the Royal Naval Hospital, Plymouth, to gain an insight into the work of Clerical and Quarters Assistants, before professional training at HMS *Raleigh*. In all, training lasts six months. Then, after 18 months' service, there is a further training period of eight weeks.

Engagement

All nurses and Clerical and Quarters assistants enrol on a nine-year notice engagement, with the right to give 18 months' notice at any time after two and a half years' service. The minimum service is four years. This initial engagement may be extended to 14 years or longer, giving entitlement to a pension on completion.

Premature Release

Premature release can be obtained for any of the following reasons:

Compassionate grounds

Invaliding if unfit

Marriage (female nurses only). Female nurses wishing to leave QARNNS to get married must give four months' notice if serving in the UK or six months' notice if serving overseas. They may remain in the Service after marriage.

Pregnancy. Women with dependent children may not remain in QARNNS.

Uniform

Both outdoor and ward uniforms are issued free, and there is an allowance to enable personnel to maintain them. Male nurses are issued with a ward uniform of white trousers and a half-sleeved white jacket. Laundering is free.

Accommodation

New entrants share a cabin with up to six others, but after six months, application may be made to live out.

Leave

Nurses and Clerical and Quarters assistants serving in the UK get 45 days' paid leave annually, with four free travel warrants.

Pay for Naval Nurses

The following table shows the monthly rates of pay for new entrants (as at 1 April 1989):

	Male	Female
RGN (Registered General Nurse) Probationary Student Nurse	£496	£492
EN(G)(Enrolled Nurse (General)) Probationary Enrolled Nurse (General)	£496	£492
QARNNS Medical Assistants On entry (under 17½)	£363	
On entry (over 17½)	£492	

QARNNS – Officers

Short service commissions are offered to nursing officers and Clerical and Quarters officers. Engagements are initially for five years with the option to leave after three years or to extend to eight years, and with the right to apply for a medium and then a full service commission.

Candidates for commissions as nursing officers should be under the age of 34 on entry, and State Registered Nurses with two years' post-registration nursing experience in a hospital.

Candidates for commissions as Clerical and Quarters officers should be between the ages of 25 and 37 on entry and should hold an HND in Hotel Catering or Institutional Management or Final Membership of the HCIMA Certificate or equivalent, and have at least one year's post-qualifying experience. Basic pay for WRNS officers and QARNNS nursing officers is as follows (as at 1 April 1989):

Probationary Third Officer (WRNS)		£9,574 per annum
Nursing Officer (QARNNS)	Male	£12,713–£14,056 per annum
	Female	£12,596–£13,928 per annum

The Royal Marines

The Royal Marines is a small corps, numbering about 7,000 men, commanded by some 600 officers. Their motto is *Per mare, per terram* (on sea and on land), which aptly describes their role. They serve as commandoes, in amphibious forces, and in HM ships. Detachments in naval ships are an integral part of their ships' companies, and their officers are encouraged to qualify for a Bridge Watch-keeping Certificate.

Joining the Royal Marines (other than Musicians)
Young men interested in joining the Royal Marines should enquire initially at the nearest Royal Navy Careers Information Office. If, after a preliminary talk with a member of staff, they decide to apply, they then return for a full interview, a written test in reasoning, English language, numeracy, and mechanical comprehension, and a medical check. If these are satisfactory, applicants take a three-day Potential Recruits Course, which is described as 'energetic, but not too tough'. The course is designed to ensure that recruits are fit enough to complete the extremely rigorous RM training, and to test their attitude to a challenge.

Junior Marines may enter between the ages of 16 and 17½. Following specialised training at the Commando Training Centre, Lympstone, they are engaged on general duties with the Royal Marine Commandoes and ships of the fleet. Royal Marines cooks and clerks receive their specialised training after completion of the Basic Commando Course.

Marines may enter from the age of 17½ up to and including the day of their 28th birthday. They undergo similar training to Junior Marines, and are employed on general duties in non-technical and technical branches. Cooks and clerks receive specialist training after completing the Basic Commando Course.

Musicians

Junior Musicians may enter the Royal Marines between the ages of 16 and 17½. They must pass an education test, interview and medical examination (which includes a dental and fitness check), as well as a test of musical aptitude. They also have an audition at the Royal Marines School of Music at Deal.

Musicians may enter from the age of 17½ up to and including the day of their 28th birthday. They must be fully-trained musicians and must pass the selection test, interview and medical examination (including dental and fitness check). They are auditioned at the Royal Marines School of Music at Deal, where they also attend a short training period before entering service with RM Bands, either ashore or afloat.

Buglers may enter as either *Junior Buglers* (between the ages of 16 and 17½), or *Adult Buglers* (between 17½ and 28). They must pass similar tests to those for Junior Musicians, after which they are trained as drummers and buglers at the Royal Marines School of Music at Deal. They then serve with RM Bands, both afloat and ashore.

Service in the Royal Marines

Royal Marine commando training lasts 30 weeks, and is very rigorous and demanding. When completed, a commando joins one of the RM commando units, but training continues on an operational basis. There are several types of unit:

Mountain and Arctic Warfare. Ready to operate in the harshest terrain, defending the frozen lands in northernmost Europe.
Jungle Warfare. Operating under hot, hostile conditions such as in Borneo.
Ships' Detachment. Sailing with the Royal Navy and trained to go ashore as a fighting force.
Air Squadron. Lifted into action by helicopter.
Special Boat Service. Skilled teams ready to be put ashore in secret to operate behind enemy lines.

The work is divided between *General Duties*, with the following specialist jobs:

Assault engineer	Driver
Landing and raiding craft crewman	Signaller
	RM policeman
Drill, platoon weapons, or PT instructor	Mountain leader
	Swimmer, canoeist
Helicopter pilot	Mortarman
Aircrewman	Anti-tank or anti-aircraft missileman
Parachutist	

and *Technical Branch*, with the following specialist jobs:

Armourer	Vehicle mechanic
Illustrator	Clerk
Metalsmith	Cook
Printer	Musician
Telecommunications technician	Bugler

Engagements

As with Royal Navy recruits, Royal Marines are entered for 22 years' service from the age of 18 or date of entry if later (see 'Terms of Engagement' in Royal Navy section on page 17).

Royal Marines Officers

Arrangements for the recruitment of officers to the Royal Marines follow the pattern of the arrangements for Royal Navy officers.

There are full career and short career commissions, the latter differing from the Royal Navy counterpart by being for four years' service with the opportunity of an extension to eight years. A gratuity is payable to short career commission officers on leaving the Service, while a full career commission carries a pension.

The ages for entry are slightly different from those set out for the Royal Navy: candidates for full career entry should be aged 17½ and under 22 on the first day of the month of entry; applicants for university cadetships should be aged 17½ and under 25 on 1 September of the year of entry; candidates for short career entry should be 17½ and under 23 on the first day of the month of entry, and direct graduate entrants for both full and short career commissions should be under the age of 25 on the first day of the month of entry.

The educational requirements for each type of entry are the same as those for candidates for Seaman, and Supply and Secretariat commissions in the Royal Navy.

All Royal Marines officers begin their service at the Commando Training Centre, Lympstone, Devon.

For details of pay and conditions, see Royal Navy section on pages 25–26.

Naval Careers Information Offices

London's area dialling code changes on 6 May 1989; 01 becomes 071 or 081.

Aberdeen
63 Belmont Street,
Aberdeen AB1 1JS (639999)

Barnsley
10 Midland Street,
Barnsley S70 1SE (242793)

Belfast
16 Howard Street,
Belfast BT1 6PA (225881)

Birmingham
Ladywood House,
45–46 Stephenson Street,
Birmingham B2 4DY
(021-632 6094)   or
46 The Pallasades,
Birmingham B2 4XD
(021-643 5552)

Blackburn
46 Church Street,
Blackburn BB1 5AL (63311)

Blackheath
9 Lee Road,
Blackheath SE3 9RQ (01-852 7988)

Brighton
83 Queen's Road
Brighton BN1 3XE (25386)

Bristol
Winterstoke Road,
Bristol BS3 2NS (664246/7) or

Esso Building,
5 Colston Avenue,
Bristol BS1 4TY (260233)

Cambridge
90–92 Regent Street,
Cambridge CB2 1DP (356970)

Canterbury
17 St. Peter's Street,
Canterbury CT1 2BG (60738)

Cardiff
The Prudential Building, Kingsway,
Cardiff CF1 4AB (225703/224897)

Carlisle
19 Warwick Road,
Carlisle CA1 1DH (23958)

Chatham
1 Dock Road,
Chatham ME4 4JR (826206)

Chelmsford
2 Park Way,
Chelmsford CM2 0SG (355134)

Coventry
First Floor, Broadgate House,
Upper Precinct,
Coventry CV1 1NU (226513)

Croydon
18 Park Street,
Croydon CR0 1YE (01-688 0489)

Derby
96 Green Lane,
Derby DE1 1RR (42691) *or*
35–36 Castlefields Main Centre,
Derby DE1 2PE (48120)

Dorchester
Georgian House, Trinity Street,
Dorchester DT1 1UD (64664)

Dundee
PO Box 81, 29–31 Bank Street,
Dundee DD1 1RW (27198)

Edinburgh
49 Lothian Road,
Edinburgh EH1 2DN
(031-229 4268/9)

Exeter
Fountain House, Western Way,
Exeter EX1 2DQ (74040)

Glasgow
Charlotte House, 78 Queen Street,
Glasgow G1 3DN (041-221 6110/9)

Guildford
20 Chertsey Street,
Guildford GU1 4HF (571465)

Hartlepool
223 York Road,
Hartlepool TS26 9AD (274040)

Hull
Town Centre House, 85 Prospect
Street, Hull HU2 8PF (25902)

Ilford
180A Cranbrook Road,
Ilford IF1 4LX (01-518 1411)

Inverness
3 Bridge Street,
Inverness IV1 1HG (233668)

Ipswich
58 Princes Street,
Ipswich IP1 1BJ (54450)

Leeds
36 Wellington Street,
Leeds LS1 2DE (458195)

Leicester
84–85 Charles Street,
Leicester LE1 1FB (20284)

Lincoln
17 Saltergate,
Lincoln LN2 1DH (25661)

Liverpool
Graeme House, Derby Square,
Liverpool L2 7SD (051-227 1764/5)

London
State House, High Holborn,
London WC1R 4TG (01-405 9951)

Luton
18–19 West Side Centre
Luton LU1 1EF (21501)

Manchester
Townbury House,
Blackfriars Street,
Salford, Manchester M3 5AF
(061-835 2916/2923)

Milton Keynes
8 Wetherburn Court,
Brunel Centre,
Milton Keynes MK2 2UH
(641094/5)

Newcastle upon Tyne
Gunner House,
Neville Street,
Newcastle upon Tyne NE1 5HD
(091-232 7048)

Northampton
13 Derngate
Northampton NN1 1TY (37518)

Norwich
45 Prince of Wales Road,
Norwich NR1 1BL (620033)

Nottingham
70 Milton Street,
Victoria Centre,
Nottingham NG1 3QX (419503)

Oxford
35 St. Giles,
Oxford OX1 3LD (53431)

Peterborough
23 Hereward Centre,
Peterborough PE1 1TB (68833)

Plymouth
105 Mayflower Street,
Plymouth PL1 1SD (266487)

Portsmouth
41 Arundel Street
Portsmouth PO1 1ND (826536)

Preston
83A Fishergate
Preston PR1 2NJ (555675)

Reading
13 Kings Road
Reading RG1 3AR (575676)

Rosyth
Orchardhead Castle Road,
Rosyth KY11 2AS (419031)

Sheffield
Castle Market,
Sheffield S1 1FZ (721476)

Shrewsbury
7–8 St. Mary's Street,
Shrewsbury SY1 1EB (232541)

Southampton
151 High Street,
Southampton SO9 4PB (223464)

St. Helens
7 George Street,
St. Helens WA10 1DA (26354)

Stoke-on-Trent
3 Charles Street, Hanley,
Stoke-on-Trent ST1 3JP (24688)

Sunderland
4 Burdon Road,
Sunderland SR1 1QB (091-514 3484)

Swansea
17–19 Castle Street,
Swansea SA1 1TE (42516)

Swindon
18 Milton Road,
Swindon SN1 5JN (34750)

Truro
Eagle Star House, 74–75 Lemon
Street, Truro TR1 2NP (73788)

Watford
35 St. Albans Road,
Watford WD1 1SH
(244055/223786)

Wolverhampton
23 Victoria Street,
Wolverhampton WV1 3PB (26433)

Worcester
44 Foregate Street,
Worcester WR1 1EE (723677)

Wrexham
21 Rhosddu Road,
Wrexham LL11 1NF (263334)

York
4 New Street,
York YO1 2RA (621543)

Chapter 3
The Army

The British Army is entirely made up of professionals – unlike some armies which rely heavily on conscripts. It is almost completely mechanised; its weapons and equipment are of the highest standard and subject to constant research and development to ensure they remain so.

The Army selects its personnel very carefully. It wants people fitted to the special sort of life which servicemen and women, and their families, have to lead. It needs men and women who can master the high-powered technology of modern weapons and equipment, and who can withstand days of active service under conditions of fatigue and hardship. It looks for people who can train hard – because army training is tough and demanding, both physically and mentally, and play hard – because the Army is keen on sport, encouraging participation in football, cricket, rugby, boxing, swimming, sailing, and virtually all other sporting activities. It places a lot of emphasis on turning its recruits into professionals of the highest calibre.

The Army exists to defend our country and its dependencies and to help maintain peace in the world. It is a part of Britain's defence system, in co-operation with the Royal Navy and the RAF. It is also a part of the allied forces within NATO (the North Atlantic Treaty Organisation), and a large part of the Army, known as the British Army of the Rhine (BAOR) is therefore stationed in Germany. This amounts to about 55,000 men and women including armour, artillery, and infantry units with support troops, who are ready for instant action to counter any threat from the East. Britain also has a brigade stationed permanently in the British sector of Berlin.

In the United Kingdom itself, the Army maintains a spearhead force ready to move at short notice to any part of the world where British interests are in danger. It also has units in Northern Ireland, assisting the Royal Ulster Constabulary in the maintenance of peace and the protection of citizens.

British soldiers may find themselves in a number of other places around the world. Military support is needed in a few remaining colonies and ex-colonies – Hong Kong, Belize, Cyprus, Gibraltar, Ascension Island and the Falkland Islands. There is also a British Army presence in Belgium, Holland, Norway, Nigeria, Zimbabwe, Uganda, Saudi Arabia, Nepal, and Brunei. Finally, the Army has training facilities in a number of friendly countries – the United States, the West Indies, Canada, Portugal, France, Denmark, Italy, Greece, Kenya, Oman, Singapore, Australia, Papua New Guinea, and New Zealand. There are therefore opportunities for soldiers to travel and see the world, and to serve at various times in greatly contrasting climatic conditions – from extreme heat to severe cold.

Organisation of the Army

The Army differs from the other two services in the way it is organised into regiments and corps. Although naval personnel are distributed among ships and shore stations, and the RAF has its stations and squadrons, these groupings in no way correspond to army regiments and corps. It has been said by foreign observers that the British Army is not so much an army as a group of regiments. This was meant disparagingly, but British soldiers are proud of their regiment or corps and would strongly oppose any attempt to alter the present system. They cherish their regiment's particular customs and peculiarities – for example, the arrangement of the buttons on their tunics, the extra cap badge of soldiers belonging to the Gloucesters, or the black bow of the Royal Welch Fusiliers. They feel they can 'belong' to a smaller organisation, while it is difficult to 'belong' to an entire army: it is the regiment which is their home. They are proud of its past achievements, and endeavour to emulate the deeds of those who served under the same colours before them. Although strong regimental loyalties have led to problems when the need has arisen to contract the Army and merge some regiments together and tact and ingenuity have been required to overcome these difficulties, by and large regimental pride and loyalty have been beneficial to the Army and to the country.

The regiments and corps which form the Army can be divided into either *Arms* or *Services*. Arms can further be divided into *Combat Arms* or *Support Arms*. These are the units which actually confront the enemy, and those who support them in the forward areas. Secondly, to back these up, are the various services which are needed to supply, equip, and generally maintain the entire army.

Although the first group of units are distinguished as combat and support arms, they both work together as a unified fighting team on the battlefield. The combat arms consist of the infantry and Royal Armoured Corps. (The ceremonial units of the Life Guards and the Blues and Royals still maintain a separate identity as Household Cavalry.) The support arms are the artillery, engineers, signals, Army Air Corps, and Intelligence Corps. Personnel of other corps, eg Field Ambulance units of the Royal Army Medical Corps, also play an important role in forward areas.

The services which back up the fighting men include the following corps:

Royal Army Medical Corps. Responsible for the treatment of the Army's sick and wounded, the maintenance of health, and the prevention of disease.

Royal Corps of Transport. Responsible for moving men, vehicles, equipment and stores by air, sea, rail and road.

Royal Army Ordnance Corps. Responsible for supplying the Army with food, fuel, equipment, weapons, tanks, missiles, etc. It also provides the Army's bomb disposal experts.

Royal Electrical and Mechanical Engineers. Responsible for the recovery, inspection, repair and modification of the Army's electronic and mechanical equipment.

Royal Military Police. Responsible for maintenance of military discipline, detection and prevention of crime, controlling traffic, etc.

Royal Army Pay Corps. Responsible for unit imprests, accounting, soldiers' pay and allowances, and financial advice.

Royal Army Veterinary Corps. Responsible for the health and training of the Army's horses and dogs.

Royal Army Dental Corps. Responsible for the dental health and hygiene of servicemen and -women worldwide, and also of their families when overseas.

Royal Army Pioneer Corps. Responsible for a variety of support tasks, such as handling stores, unloading ships, etc.

Intelligence Corps. Responsible for collecting and analysing intelligence material about an enemy; also for security and counter-intelligence.

Army Catering Corps. Responsible for feeding the army in barracks and in the field; also for catering for special occasions.

RANKS	
Army	**WRAC**
Field Marshal	
General	
Lieutenant-General	
Major-General	
Brigadier	Brigadier
Colonel	Colonel
Lieutenant-Colonel	Lieutenant-Colonel
Major	Major
Captain	Captain
Lieutenant	Lieutenant
2nd Lieutenant	2nd Lieutenant
Warrant Officer I (Regtl. Sergeant-Major)	Warrant Officer I
Warrant Officer II (Company Sergeant-Major)	Warrant Officer II
Colour Sergeant	Staff Sergeant
Sergeant	Sergeant
Corporal	Corporal
Lance-Corporal	Lance-Corporal
Private (Guardsman, Gunner, Sapper, etc.)	Private

The names of various army ranks differ between regiments, eg the Household Cavalry do not use the title 'Sergeant', but 'Corporal of Horse' instead.

The Army Careers Information Office (AC10)
Information about the various regiments and corps of the Army can be obtained from the nearest Army Careers Information Office (for the address, consult your telephone book). Here you will find information about entry into either commissioned or non-commissioned rank, into the Women's Royal Army Corps and Queen Alexandra's Royal Army Nursing Corps. You can enquire without being placed under any pressure to enlist, but those who are really interested in doing so can discuss the options open to them (including the army trade in which they might specialise) and will be informed of the

various steps to be taken before attestation. Everyone wishing to join the Forces must satisfy three requirements: nationality, physical fitness, and educational ability (see Chapter 1 for details).

Recruitment of Other (ie Non-Officer) Ranks (Male)

A serious applicant is interviewed by the Army Careers Office staff to determine, first of all, why he wishes to join the Army, and what he hopes to get out of it. Further questioning about his interests, educational achievements and previous experience is designed to ascertain which regiment or corps would be the most suitable for him. The careers staff test his intelligence, give him a preliminary medical examination, and gradually assess his suitability for an army career.

These preliminaries are not rushed. An applicant may then be formally interviewed by a Personnel Selection Officer or ACO before being finally accepted. At this stage, a few applicants have to be told, with regret, that they are clearly not suited to the Army and would not be happy there. They are sympathetically advised to seek a career elsewhere. It sometimes becomes clear to an applicant himself that he is making a mistake in thinking of the Army, and sometimes an applicant receives the offer of a civilian job which he feels gives better prospects: in either event, he is at perfect liberty to withdraw his application.

The Army Personnel Selection Centre (APSC)

Although the careers staff may reject an applicant because of his unsuitability, it is not up to them to accept candidates who appear to be suitable. Until 1990, this decision is made only after applicants have spent a day at the Army Personnel Selection Centre, Sutton Coldfield, and undergone a number of further tests. These include a run of about a mile to see what sort of physical shape applicants are in, and an assortment of physical exercises in the gym. It is most important to make sure that recruits can stand up to the basic combat training every soldier has to undergo, irrespective of what trade he might be entering.

The centre is, in fact, a foretaste of army life. Applicants have to keep their rooms tidy, even though they are there for such a short time, and they are marched about to the various classrooms, gyms, etc just as if they were already enlisted soldiers. They are assessed throughout the visit by one of the centre's personnel selection officers, who weighs up how each applicant has fared in the physical tests, and interviews each one again in a follow-up of the earlier interview at the ACIO. Applicants are asked a lot of personal questions, necessary for the selection staff to get to know them fully, and finally the decision is taken as to who will be offered places in the Army. From April 1990, this assessment and the decision will be taken by PSOs at the ACIO.

Age

Young people may join at the age of 16 as members of the Junior Army. Nearly a third of all recruits are very young, and many of today's senior officers entered at an early age. Boys of 15 may apply. If they are suitable, they are given an acceptance certificate which guarantees them a place in the Army when they leave school, but does not bind them if they decide not to do so. This is known as the *Guaranteed Vacancy Scheme*.

There are three grades of boy entrant: those who have potential skills may become *Army Apprentices*; those with the makings of NCOs become *Junior Leaders*; the remainder become either *Junior Soldiers* or *Junior Bandsmen*.

Army Apprentices

Boys should be between the ages of 15 years 11 months and 17½ and have their parents' consent to apply. They must also be fit. The type of apprenticeship for which they will be selected depends upon their educational attainments.

To be *technician apprentices* they should have obtained or be capable of obtaining suitable grades at GCSE/GCE O level (or equivalent) in mathematics, English, and either physics or an engineering subject. They should also have the potential to reach the Business and Technician Education Council (BTEC) National Certificate or Diploma in Engineering (roughly of GCE A-level standard) during their two years' apprenticeship.

There are a number of choices available to those seeking a technician apprenticeship. The *Royal Engineers* train their apprentices at the Army Apprentices College, Chepstow. The trades are in three groups:

1. *Design Technicians:*
   Construction Materials   Design Draughtsman
      Technician   Draughtsman Electrical and
   Surveyor Engineering   Mechanical
2. *Survey Technicians:*
   Field Survey Technician   Survey Photographic
   Air Survey Technician   Technician
   Survey Cartographic Technician Survey Print Technician
3. *Electricians RE*

The Royal Corps of Signals train their apprentices at the Army Apprentices College, Harrogate. The trades are as follows:

Electronics Technicians:
   Radio Technician   Terminal Equipment
   Radio Relay Technician   Technician

The Royal Corps of Transport also train their apprentices at the Army Apprentices College, Chepstow, in one trade:

Marine Engineer:
   The final part of the course is on board ship with the Maritime Division of the School of Transportation, Gosport. While at Chepstow, apprentices undertake a 10-day cruise on an RCT vessel for on-board training.

The Corps of Royal Electrical and Mechanical Engineers train their apprentices at the Princess Marina College, Arborfield, near Reading. The trades are in three groups:

1. *Electronics Technicians:*
   Telecommunications   Control Equipment
      Technician   Technician
   Radar Technician   Avionics Technician
2. *Aircraft Technicians*
3. *Instrument Technicians*

To be *craft apprentices*, applicants should have obtained or be capable of obtaining suitable grades at GCSE/O level (or equivalent) in mathematics, English, and either physics or an engineering subject. They should also have the potential to reach City and Guilds of London Institute Part 2 Examination standard during their two years' apprenticeship.

Trades include armourer, gun fitter, vehicle electrician (two-year courses) and metalsmith and vehicle mechanic (one-year courses).

Apprenticeships are also available in a number of supporting trades. Courses last for one year and applicants should have satisfactorily completed five years' secondary education.

Curriculum at Apprentices Colleges
Each year at an Apprentices College is divided into three 14-week terms with half-term breaks. In a normal week, the programme of formal training from Monday to Friday covers about 30 hours, with mid-morning and mid-afternoon breaks and one hour for lunch. It is varied and includes technical training, education, military and physical training, religious education, and sports. On Saturday morning, apprentices take part in regimental training activities and occasional ceremonial parades.

Leadership and character-building are an important part of apprentice training: apprentices can expect to become NCOs before long, and will have to control and motivate men in their charge. From time to time, they are taken out of the familiar college surroundings to some remote part of Scotland, Wales, or the North York Moors. Here they live rough, sleep rough, cook their own meals, and tramp long distances carrying heavy packs. They take turns at leading a team in a tactical exercise. Other outdoor exercises are designed to teach apprentices to handle the equipment they are being trained to repair and maintain under difficult active service conditions.

Supporting trade apprentices are fully integrated into their college programmes. Their time is spent on education, military and leadership training, and trade-associated training. However, the bulk of their trade training is taught after they have completed the three terms at the Apprentices College and enter one of the adult training units.

Leave between terms is normally three weeks at the end of the spring term, four weeks in the summer, and three at Christmas. Apprentices receive four free railway warrants each year, and while the Ministry of Defence contract with British Rail is in operation, they are issued with Forces railcards entitling them to half-fare travel.

Accommodation
College accommodation is modern, centrally heated, and well equipped. Apprentices sleep no more than eight to a room, and some rooms are occupied by four only. All accommodation affords a considerable degree of privacy and some senior apprentices may have single rooms. There are baths, showers, toilets and service rooms with washing-machines and facilities for drying, ironing and cleaning.

A modern kitchen provides a good choice of food.

Pay
During their first term, apprentices are required to open a current bank account. Pay is credited directly to their accounts, monthly in arrears. During the early terms, apprentices are given instruction in the management of their personal financial affairs and encouraged to start saving through a building society.

Compulsory Evening Activities
Apprentices are encouraged to make the best use of their time by pursuing an activity on one evening every week. This is compulsory during the first year, but voluntary thereafter. Expert instructors are provided in a wide range of hobbies and activities. Apprentices are also encouraged to devote some time to voluntary service, such as helping in the maintenance of children's playgrounds, organising functions for disabled persons, etc. Those with musical abilities or aspirations may find a place in their college band.

Promotion
While at college an apprentice may be promoted, first to Apprentice Lance-Corporal, and subsequently through ascending ranks to Apprentice Regimental Sergeant Major. Apprentice NCOs assist the adult sergeants and corporals, and the Apprentice RSM takes the passing-out parade. These apprentice ranks only hold good during the time at college. They are relinquished as soon as an apprentice joins the adult army.

Once an apprentice has qualified as a technician in some trades, he may be given the rank of Lance-Corporal when he joins his adult unit, provided his company commander at college has certified his readiness for promotion. Further promotion to Corporal may be expected after a further six months. Promotion to Sergeant depends upon success at a higher training course, and subsequently, after additional courses, a man may achieve the rank of Staff Sergeant or Warrant Officer.

Artificers
From the age of 23 onwards, tradesmen may be selected for training as Engineer Artificers. This brings automatic promotion to staff sergeant at the end of approximately 18 months' specialist training. During this period, selected tradesmen are afforded the opportunity

to qualify for a Business and Technician Education Council (BTEC) Higher National Certificate, thus gaining Technician Engineer status. They are then eligible for further promotion to warrant officer, and those who display exceptional qualities of leadership and management may earn consideration for a commission.

Artificer Entry Scheme
The Army has special arrangements for men who have already served an apprenticeship in a mechanical, electrical or electronics trade and have reached ONC or equivalent standard. Such men, if they are between the ages of 23 and 30, may enlist as artificers to fill supervisory appointments. Those accepted after interview enter the Army as sergeants and are given 15 months' further training. After this is completed successfully, they are promoted to staff sergeant.

Junior Leaders
Recruits between the ages of 15 years 11 months and 17 who show the potential to become NCOs or warrant officers, particularly in front-line units, may be chosen at the Army Personnel Selection Centre to train as junior leaders. Those so selected are sent to join a junior leader regiment, of which there are several. Some take boys who are all intended for one particular arm. Others are for boys who are preparing for various regiments and corps. Much of the training, which can last up to 16 months, follows the same pattern in all regiments: map-reading, fieldcraft, the use of small arms, adventure training and extended camps. Boys are encouraged to improve their education and prepare for GCSE and other relevant examinations. They are also taught military skills appropriate to their intended arm.

Junior Soldiers
Boys who are not selected to become junior leaders may join as junior soldiers. They undergo very similar training, but normally their course lasts only one year. Those who need to reach a basic educational standard might be sent on an Army Preliminary Education course which is run by officers of the Royal Army Education Corps.

The Army also trains junior musicians and junior bandsmen. Previous musical training is desirable, but not essential, provided that boys have an ear for music and an aptitude for learning to play an instrument. Training takes up to two years and includes further general education. Boys showing special ability may be sent on a year's course to the Royal School of Military Music. Infantry regiments train junior drummers and buglers, while Scottish and Irish regiments train pipers.

Young Soldiers

Boys who are too old to enter as juniors may, if they are under the age of 17½, enlist as young soldiers. If they subsequently realise they are unsuited to army life they may leave without penalty during their first six months.

Junior Entrants' Engagements

All junior entrants (apprentices, junior leaders and junior soldiers) enlist on a notice engagement. This means that they agree to serve from the time they join their unit until their 18th birthday and then for either six or nine years beyond that date, depending on the training they choose. If within the first six months of service they realise they are not suited to army life, they can leave without cost. Once they reach the age of 18, they have the chance to review the time they agreed to serve when they enlisted. They may reduce their six- or nine-year agreement to three years, running from their 18th birthday or from the end of their training – whichever is the later.

Adult Entry

Adults normally enlist between the ages of 17½ and 25. Acceptance by particular arms depends upon a recruit's physical fitness, intelligence and capabilities. Combat arms require men of Grade A (peak) standard of fitness. The main supporting corps require Grade B. Other corps will accept men of Grades C or D. The Army also grades recruits according to their level of intelligence. Some units will only accept men who have scored very highly in the intelligence tests. Others will take those with lower scores.

Adult Engagements

Most recruits enlist under a notice engagement. Under this, they agree to serve for a period of 22 years from their 18th birthday, or from the date of joining their unit if this is later. They have certain rights with regard to giving notice to leave. Once they have completed 18 months' service they may at any time give 18 months' notice of their intention to leave. Once they have completed three years with the colours, ie actually serving in the Army, they may terminate their service at any time, provided they give 12 months' notice.

Some modification of these rules apply to trades involving lengthy training, however. Men in these trades have to complete four and a half or seven and a half years before they can give notice, depending on their trade. Similarly, instead of having to complete only three years before being eligible to give 12 months' notice, they have to serve either six or nine years, depending on the trade they follow.

Some recruits commit themselves to six or nine years' colour service at the time they enlist. By so doing, they earn the right to a higher rate of pay. Of course, soldiers can carry on and complete their full engagement of 22 years and thus earn a full pension.

Special Regiments and Formations

The Guards Division consists of five regiments: the Grenadier, Coldstream, Scots, Irish, and Welsh Guards. The first three consist of two battalions, and the last two of only one. Usually, three of the eight battalions are serving overseas (as a rule with BAOR, or in Berlin), one is doing a tour of duty in Northern Ireland, and four are based in London. The Guards Division has its depot at Pirbright Camp in Surrey, where all guardsmen undergo their initial training. There is also an adventure training camp in Devon and a battle camp in Norfolk. When on ceremonial duty, guardsmen are housed either in Wellington Barracks, Birdcage Walk, London, or in Victoria Barracks, Windsor.

The Household Cavalry consists of two regiments: the Life Guards and the Blues and Royals. They recruit from all over the United Kingdom (unlike the foot guards, each regiment of which has its own recruiting area). Almost one-fifth of the Household Cavalry is engaged on ceremonial duties. The remainder forms two service regiments, one of which is equipped with tanks, while the other has a reconnaissance role and is equipped with light tanks and scout cars. These regiments serve mainly in Germany.

New recruits are trained initially at Pirbright, where they spend 22 weeks learning drill, weapons and fieldcraft, etc. They then opt to begin training, either in the mounted or the armoured section. They are under no compulsion to do mounted training, but most recruits opt to do this immediately, before serving at least two years in the mounted section. Training in the armoured section is undertaken at Catterick in North Yorkshire.

Commando Gunners are selected volunteers from the Royal Artillery who work with the Royal Navy and Royal Marine commandos.

They are based at Plymouth, Poole and Arbroath, but are ready to operate anywhere in the world. Their job is to act as the eyes of the Navy when warships are firing at land targets. In the Falklands conflict, they went ashore five days ahead of the landings at San Carlos and directed the Navy to pour shells on the Argentinian defences.

Another special formation of volunteers are the *Parachute Gunners*, who belong to the Field Regiment based at Aldershot. They are carefully selected and receive intensive parachute training with the Parachute Regiment.

The Parachute Regiment came into existence in August 1942, since when it has won renown in many theatres of war – most recently in the Falkland Islands when two of its three battalions (2 Para and 3 Para) played leading roles. The regiment is very selective and will only accept the very fittest men and those with high intelligence scores. Before proceeding to the Parachute Training School at RAF Abingdon, recruits are put through a very gruelling course of adventure and battle training which weeds out about one man in eight. After four weeks' parachute training, recruits take part in two airborne exercises in the final two weeks of their initial training.

The Special Air Service (SAS) was created in 1952 when a special force was needed to operate against Communist terrorists in Malaya. Since then, the SAS has been used in several parts of the world and for several special tasks: in Borneo, between 1962 and 1966, during the confrontation with Indonesia; in Oman between 1965 and 1977, when the sultan requested help to suppress a rebellion; in London, to free hostages held at the Iranian embassy; in Northern Ireland and Gibraltar against the IRA. Sometimes the SAS is used in an advisory capacity, such as when another country needs help in dealing with a hijacking or other form of terrorism.

It is not possible to join the SAS direct: it recruits from other units of the Army – largely, but not entirely, from the Parachute Regiment. On joining, all soldiers (except officers) lose their rank and become plain troopers. They then begin some of the toughest training imaginable, beginning with 14 weeks of hard physical effort, combat survival and parachute training. They then receive further training in signalling, medical aid, explosives, demolition, and jungle warfare. After a probationary year, they are sent on advanced training in mountaineering, skiing, underwater swimming, and radio work. Languages are also studied, and between them, members of the SAS have knowledge of a wide range of languages.

The SAS is a small unit which usually operates in teams of four. Each man in the team can do any of the jobs required by the mission, but each has a special responsibility for some role in which he is particularly expert. Men of the SAS keep a low profile, as was demonstrated at the Gibraltar inquest in 1988 into the shooting of three IRA terrorists. They never assist a possible enemy by allowing their names or photographs to appear in the press, or by appearing in public as acknowledged SAS men.

The Army Air Corps is one of the newest corps in the Army. Its helicopters are essential for modern warfare in their reconnaissance and observer roles. The Corps was also used in the Falklands for ferrying supplies to forward areas and bringing out casualties. A helicopter crew consists of a pilot, an observer, and an air gunner, but it needs ground support from drivers, signallers, clerks and other personnel to load, marshal and fuel the aircraft. The Corps' depot is at Middle Wallop, but recruits do their basic training at Catterick, with driver-training at Leconfield.

Detailed information about the regiments and corps of the British Army can be obtained from Army Careers Information Offices. Most regiments have museums in their home towns which are well worth a visit. They contain the story of a regiment's beginnings, its history and its present role, set out in graphic displays assisted by models and videos. There is also a background of time-honoured uniforms, flags and mementoes from the many campaigns and overseas tours of duty which are the highlights of every regiment's story.

Rates of pay for Soldiers (as at 1 April 1989)

Weekly Rates

Junior Entrants aged 16–16½	£63.70
aged 16½–17	£71.12
aged 17–17½	£83.31
aged 17½ and over while in Junior training	£114.17
Young Soldiers aged 17–17½	£86.31

In the following table, Scale A is for soldiers committed to serving for less than six years; Scale B for soldiers committed for six years but less than nine; Scale C is for soldiers committed for nine years or more.

Adults	Band	Scale A	Scale B	Scale C
Private over 17½ on entry	1	£114.17	£116.27	£119.42
Private Class III	1	£126.70	£128.80	£131.45
Private Class II	1	£141.82	£143.92	£147.07
Private Class I	1	£153.93	£156.03	£159.18
Lance-Corporal Class 1	1	£179.06	£181.16	£184.31
Corporal Class 1	2	£227.85	£229.95	£233.31
Sergeant	5			£254.03
Staff Sergeant	5			£267.05
Warrant Officer Class II	6			£308.35
Warrant Officer Class I	7			£352.03

Rates of Pay for Army Officers (as at 1 April 1989)

Rank	On appointment	Rising to
University Cadetships	£6,001	£8,275
University Bursary	£1,200	
Short Service Limited Commission	£7,245	£7,742
Officer Cadet	£6,782	
Second Lieutenant	£9,662	
Lieutenant	£12,713	£14,056
Captain	£16,184	£18,812
Major	£20,404	£24,433
Lieutenant Colonel	£28,050	£30,999
Colonel	£32,346	£35,748
Brigadier	£38,748	

Officers

There are three main types of commission in the Army for the younger entrant:

    Regular Commission (Reg C)
    Special Regular Commission (Young or Middle Entry)
        (SRC (YE and ME))
    Short Service Commission (SSC)

Regular Commission

A regular commission (Reg C) may be granted to young men who have just left school or university and who from the outset wish to make the Army their career.

The educational requirements are:

☐ *Non-graduates*. Passes in five approved subjects which must normally include English, mathematics and either a science subject or a foreign language at GCSE/O level, with two passes at A level (or equivalent) for direct entry on the Reg C list.

☐ *Graduates*. Any UK university or CNAA degree is acceptable. Membership of certain professional institutions is acceptable for the Royal Artillery, the Royal Engineers, and the Royal Signals. An approved degree or qualification accepted by Ministry of Defence as equivalent is required for the Royal Army Educational Corps (RAEC).

Further details are outlined in the pamphlet *Graduates in the Army*, obtainable from:

> Ministry of Defence (DAR 1a) (A),
> Empress State Building,
> Lillie Road,
> London SW6 1TR

For a Reg C in the Royal Electrical and Mechanical Engineers (REME), a degree acceptable to one of the following institutions is required:

> Institution of Electrical Engineers
> Institution of Electronic and Radio Engineers
> Institution of Mechanical Engineers
> Royal Aeronautical Society
> Institution of Production Engineers

Reg C officers can expect to have a career to the age of 55. They are not normally allowed to leave the Army less than three years from the date of their commission. Thereafter, they may normally apply to leave at any time on giving a minimum of seven months' notice. However, officers who have taken a degree course within the Army, a staff college course, and certain other longer courses are required to serve longer periods before they may apply to leave.

On resignation or retirement, officers may be eligible for retired pay and terminal awards. They are also required to transfer to the Regular Army Reserve of Officers.

Special Regular Commission

A special regular commission may be granted to civilians, including retired officers of the three services or of the Commonwealth forces, and to serving soldiers in the British Army. The commission is initially for a period of 16 years on the Active List.

The SRC is designed for applicants who would have liked to apply for a regular commission but were not eligible to do so because they were over the age limit or had not achieved two GCE A-level passes. It is divided into two categories:

1. SRC (Young Entry). This commission is for applicants who do not achieve satisfactory grades at A level and are therefore not eligible for a Reg C. They are required to have passed through the same educational stages as a Reg C applicant and must have completed a full A-level or equivalent course. The normal upper age limit is 22 years on entry to Sandhurst.

2. SRC (Middle Entry). This is for applicants between the ages of 22 and 29 (26 for some arms and 29 for others) who are too old, or below the educational standard for Reg C.

The educational requirements for a SRC are as follows:

☐ *SRC (Young Entry).* Passes at GCSE (or equivalent) in a minimum of five approved subjects, which must normally include English, mathematics, and either a science subject or a foreign language. Direct entry may also be awarded to candidates with a minimum of two low-grade passes at A level.

☐ *SRC (Middle Entry).* Passes at GCSE (or equivalent) in a minimum of five approved subjects, including English and mathematics (and for the Royal Engineers and Royal Signals, a science subject).

The requirements for REME and the RAEC are as set out for Reg C Commissions above.

The SRC is initially for a period of 16 years' commissioned service. Extensions may be granted for one, two, or three years at a time, depending on foreseeable employment and on the officer's wishes. Service is not permitted beyond the age of 55. SRC Officers (except those in the Army Air Corps) are eligible to apply for conversion to a Reg C after a minimum of 24 months' commissioned service.

SRC officers are not normally allowed to leave the Army less than three years from the date of their commission. Thereafter, they may normally apply to leave at any time on giving a minimum of seven months' notice; officers who have been on lengthy courses in the Army are required to serve longer (see Reg C above). Conditions for resignation or retirement are similar to those for Reg C officers.

Short Service Commission

Young men who have not yet decided on a career are invited to join the Army on a short service commission for a period of three years (or longer if they wish) when they leave school or university. The SSC is also available to those leaving school who have a guaranteed place at university (see below for undergraduate awards).

The educational requirements for an SSC are as follows:

- [ ] *Non-graduates.* Passes at GCSE/O level (or equivalent) in five subjects to include English. The Royal Engineers require mathematics and a science, the Royal Signals mathematics and physics, the Army Air Corps, Royal Army Ordnance Corps and Royal Army Pay Corps mathematics. REME applicants should be qualified to read for an engineering degree. REAC applicants should hold a teaching certificate or an approved degree or qualification accepted by the Ministry of Defence.
- [ ] *Graduates.* A UK university or CNAA degree, or (for certain corps) membership of certain professional institutions.

Short service commissions are initially for a period of three years, but may be extended to a maximum of seven years 364 days. Those commissioned into the Army Air Corps are committed to serve for a minimum of six years. After 24 months' service, an SSC may apply to convert to a Reg C or SRC. It is possible for an officer to leave after only two years, without a gratuity, if he so wishes.

Applying for a Commission

It is important that an applicant is advised and sponsored by an expert as soon as he begins to consider a commission. This is normally done by a schools liaison officer (SLO), university liaison officer (ULO), the army careers officer (ACO) in the area where the applicant lives, or by the recruiting officer of the arm or corps which the applicant is interested in joining. SLOs and ULOs visit schools and universities and are readily available to give advice. If an applicant does not know who to contact, he should write to the MOD (DAR 1a) (A) (address on page 58). Application Forms AFB 6610 and F/Ident/177 should be obtained from whoever is advising or sponsoring.

Pre-Regular Commissions Board Briefings
A candidate whose application is accepted will be required to attend an Army Medical Board. The sponsoring officer will then arrange a Pre-Regular Commissions Board Briefing, run by many military establishments throughout the country and lasting two days. The applicant will be advised whether

   (a) he is suitable to go straight to the Regular Commissions Board (RCB), or

   (b) he should do an 8 to 10 week GCSE-type course to enhance his chances, or

   (c) he is not considered suitable.

The Regular Commissions Board
After attending an Army Medical Board and a Pre-RCB Briefing, the candidate will be called to the RCB at Westbury, Wiltshire, for tests of personality and leadership. Successful candidates proceed to the Royal Military Academy, Sandhurst.

Short Service Limited Commissions

These commissions are designed for young men *and women* who have left school and wish to spend a year gaining experience before going on to university or polytechnic. Those who pass the rigorous selection procedures at the RCB attend a three-week course at Sandhurst, either in January or November, and are commissioned into their chosen corps or regiments as 2nd Lieutenants on a special rate of pay. They serve for a minimum of four months with a front-line unit (although not where active service operations are in progress), ending their service shortly before entering university. Thereafter, there are no reserve liabilities whatever, and no subsequent obligation to serve in the Army. Those who decide after graduation to return to the Army for an SSC or full career will not normally have to repeat the full selection procedure.

To be eligible for an SSLC, applicants must have a firm or conditional place at a UK university or polytechnic to read for a recognised first degree. Final acceptance will depend on all necessary academic work and examinations having been completed and the university or polytechnic place confirmed before entry to Sandhurst. Candidates must be recommended by a headmaster or headmistress, have reached the age of 18 years and be under 20 years on the day of commissioning, and be unmarried. They must also be accepted by the corps or regiment of their choice, and satisfy the Army's high medical standards. Finally, they must have passed the Regular Commissions Board with a special recommendation for SSLC.

Army Undergraduate Awards

Up to half the officers now entering the Army are graduates, and the majority take advantage of sponsorship schemes: the Army Undergraduate Cadetship and the Army Undergraduate Bursary.

Army Undergraduate Cadetship. This is designed for young men *or women* who decide before entering university or early on in their degree course that they wish to make a career as an Army officer and to serve for at least five years after graduation. After passing the selection procedure, they join a short course at Sandhurst just before going to university (or for those already there, during the long vacation). Cadets are commissioned on probation, and paid as officers throughout the degree course. On completion, graduates return to Sandhurst for a graduate course, at the end of which the regular commission is confirmed.

Cadetships are only awarded to candidates who are well above average in academic and leadership ability. They can be awarded at any time up to the beginning of the final year of a degree course but are effective only after successful completion of the course at Sandhurst, which is held annually in early September.

Army Bursary Scheme. This is for undergraduates, both men *and women*, who wish to commit themselves to the minimum of a three-year short service commission. The Army provides financial support and opportunities for paid training, which supplement the normal LEA grant and other sources of student income. In exchange, the bursary-holder undertakes to serve a minimum of three years as an officer after completion of the course at Sandhurst.

During the degree course the Army requires nothing beyond reasonable academic attainment, although nearly all bursary-holders voluntarily carry out part-time training with the University Officers' Training Corps and vacation training attachments to their parent units in the UK and overseas. Such voluntary training attracts extra pay and allowances. Bursaries can be awarded at any time up to the beginning of the final year of a degree course, and can be effective from the beginning of the next academic term.

As with candidates for a cadetship, candidates for a bursary must have a confirmed place at a university or polytechnic. They must be over 17½ years of age on 1 September of the year of entry and expect to graduate before their 25th birthday. They must be unmarried and able to meet the required medical standards.

Applications to these schemes should be made as detailed in the section 'Applying for a Commission' on page 60. (See also the booklet *Army Undergraduate Awards* CP(A)31.)

The Army Scholarship Scheme

The Army holds two competitions annually (in spring and autumn) at each of which 45 scholarships are awarded. This is designed to attract boys of the highest ability into a career as a Regular Army officer by giving financial assistance to parents or guardians towards the cost of the last two years of school education. During this time, the boy remains at school to study for GCE A levels or equivalent, which must be at the standard required for entry to Sandhurst or to university under the Army's Undergraduate Awards Scheme. Successful scholars are exempt from attending the Regular Commissions Board and are guaranteed a regular commission, provided they reach the necessary educational standard. They also have to be medically fit and complete their Sandhurst training successfully.

Candidates must normally be between the ages of 16 and 16½ on 1 January for the spring competition and 1 July for the autumn competition. For full details, see the booklet *Army Scholarship Scheme* (CP(A)29).

Graduate Direct Entry (Men and Women)

In addition to graduates who enter the Army through one of the schemes mentioned above, there are many who only decide to enter after graduation. They are commissioned as Graduate Direct Entrants.

Broadly speaking, most branches of the Army accept graduates in any degree discipline, but certain corps and regiments require specific qualifications. (Details of these can be obtained from the Army booklet *Graduate Direct Entry* CP(A)32.) Age limits vary according to type of commission and the corps or regiment applied for, and are as follows:

(a) Regular commissions: Under 23 for Intelligence Corps; under 25 for RAC, Infantry, AAC, RCT, RAOC, RMP, RAPC, RAEC, RPC, ACC; under 29 for RA, RE, R. Signals, WRAC; and under 30 for REME.

(b) Special regular commissions and short service commissions:

under 26 for RAC, Infantry, AAC, RMP; under 30 for REME; under 29 for all others. Not applicable to Intelligence Corps.

(c) Applicants for WRAC for permanent employment with other corps must conform to the appropriate corps age limit.

All candidates must be passed by an Army Medical Board.

Applications should be made as detailed above, and the selection procedure follows that already described. All graduate direct entrants are required to attend a seven months' graduate course at the Royal Military Academy, Sandhurst. Female graduates attend a similar course at the WRAC Wing, Sandhurst. On the successful completion of the course, a graduate's commission is confirmed.

Specialist Services

There are special requirements for entry to certain branches of the Army:

(a) *Royal Army Chaplain's Department*. Graduate clergy should normally have served at least one curacy, and should be under the age of 34.

(b) *Royal Army Medical Corps*. Direct entry for Reg C, SRC, or SSC is open to all qualified medical practitioners. Medical cadetships may be awarded to selected candidates (male and female) who have passed their second MB or equivalent examination, who have started clinical studies, or who are within three years of qualification below the age of 25.

(c) *Royal Army Veterinary Corps*. Qualified veterinary graduates under 42 years of age may apply.

(d) *Royal Army Dental Corps*. Direct entry for Reg C, SRC and SSC is open to qualified dental practitioners. Dental cadetships may be awarded to dental students (male or female) who are within the final two years of studies.

(e) *Army Legal Corps*. Commissions in the rank of Captain may be awarded to qualified solicitors or barristers between the ages of 24 and 30.

Fuller details of entry to these specialist corps may be obtained from the Ministry of Defence (address on page 58).

The Women's Royal Army Corps

The first step for women who are interested in joining the Women's Royal Army Corps (WRAC) is to contact their nearest Army Careers Information Office and have a talk with the personnel there. The procedure is similar to that for men which is described on p. 47. After taking the Army entrance test and passing a medical examination, applicants are asked to consider what jobs they would prefer to be trained for, and to make a choice of three. In due course, they are called for interview and assessment at the WRAC Selection Centre, Queen Elizabeth Park, Guildford, Surrey. This assessment takes two days, after which suitable applicants are offered a vacancy, and told when they might expect to start training. About a month before this date, they are called again to the Army Careers Information Office where they are asked to confirm that they still wish to enter the WRAC. Only when they do so are they finally enlisted. This delay in the actual commencement of training is a deliberate policy designed to ensure that applicants are really committed to their decision.

Choice of Trade
The minimum age for applications is 17 years and 3 months. The initial engagement is for three years, but this can be extended. The following trades are available, and training in a trade follows the seven weeks' basic training all new recruits receive at the WRAC Centre:

Administration Assistant. May work in an office or stores. Office work consists of general clerical duties and filing; stores work involves the issue and storage of equipment and clothing, dealing with laundry, dry cleaning and shoe repairs. Some administration assistants act as *Regimental Policewomen*.

Analyst (Special Intelligence). Trained and employed by the Intelligence Corps on detailed clerical work. GCSEs/O levels in English, mathematics and a foreign language preferred. Women with an aptitude for languages have opportunities to train as *Linguist (Special Intelligence)*.

Clerk. Duties include touch-typing, filing, dealing with mail, documentation, photocopying, answering the telephone, and generally assisting in the running of an office. Women who can already type, or who have had previous experience of audio-typing or taking shorthand, may be selected for extra training as *Clerk Typist*, *Audio Typist*, or *Shorthand Writer*.

Cook. Duties include all aspects of catering. Cooks work a shift system. Opportunities exist to gain City and Guilds Certificates at the end of the training course.

Data Telegraphist. Works with the Royal Signals receiving, processing and transmitting signal messages, using both teleprinters and tape-relay equipment.

Driver. Trained to drive a variety of vehicles including Land Rovers, minibuses and four-ton trucks to HGV3 level. Instructed in basic maintenance and fault-finding, map reading and vehicle documentation.

Kennelmaid. Works with the Royal Army Veterinary Corps at Melton Mowbray in Leicestershire. Duties include grooming, exercising and feeding army dogs. Previous experience of working with dogs essential.

Medical Assistant. Gives minor treatment, administers medicine, acts as receptionist, clerk and nursing attendant in the unit medical centre.

Military Accountant. Employed by the Royal Army Pay Corps on clerical work, dealing with soldiers' pay and allowances.

Military Policewoman. Works alongside Royal Military Police and receives the same training. Duties include foot and mobile patrols, crowd and traffic control, security checks, advising and assisting members of the Forces and general public. Trained to drive and instructed in self-defence.

Movement Controller. Assists in the direction and control of use of all types of transport. Employed at ports, airfields, railway terminals and road-heads, with responsibility for the safe movement of people and cargo.

Musician. Applicants must be competent to play one instrument used by military bands. Should have reached Grade 6 in main instrument and will be auditioned by the Director of Music before being accepted. All bandswomen are also trained as Medical Assistants. The WRAC Staff Band is based at the WRAC Centre in Guildford.

Operator Intelligence and Security. Trained and employed by the Intelligence Corps. Usually works as part of a small security detachment concerned with security of documents, personnel and equipment. The preferred qualifications are GCSE/O level passes in English with two passes from mathematics, a science, a language, history or geography.

Physical Training Instructor. Responsible for all types of physical and recreational training – team games, athletics, swimming, adventure training, orienteering, etc. Able to coach, umpire and instruct. Previous experience is essential. Recruits required to pass a special selection board.

Postal and Courier Operator. Receives, sorts and despatches forces' mail. Handles registered, insured and classified mail. Shift work is usually involved.

Range Assistant. Trained and employed by the Royal Artillery. Primarily concerned with range safety. Work involves operation of air/sea surveillance radars and radio communications; the manning of control consoles; maintenance of equipment; computer operation; knowledge of missile safety systems; setting up of launcher behaviour cameras, and of ultraviolet and video tape recorders. Only two postings: Benbecula in the Hebrides and Lulworth in Dorset.

Stewardess. May be employed in officers' or sergeants' mess or in junior ranks dining-hall. Lays tables, serves food and drinks, may look after officers' accommodation and uniforms.

Supply Controller. Works with Royal Army Ordnance Corps. Duties include paperwork side of storekeeping, dealing with issue and receipt vouchers, invoices, ledgers, and stock control. Those with punch-card or comptometer experience have the opportunity to train as *Operator Computer Machine*.

Supply Specialist. Works with Royal Army Ordnance Corps. Concerned with receipt and inspection of items from manufacturers, their storage and preservation, also their selection and packing for issue to units. Deals with all types of equipment – clothing, vehicle spares, stationery, ammunition, etc.

Switchboard Operator. Trained and employed by the Royal Signals. Works on military telephone exchanges, routing and connecting calls, recognising and reporting faults, taking messages, etc. Must be prepared to work shifts.

Terminal Equipment Technician. Works with the Royal Signals as communications system engineer helping to install, use, faultfind, repair, modify and test equipment, ranging from teleprinters and telephone exchanges to radio exchanges. Preferably, applicants should have two GCSE/O-level passes, among them English, mathematics or physics, and enjoy working with their hands.

Conditions in the WRAC
Accommodation is provided in a modern centrally-heated building.

New entrants usually have to share a room with three other girls, but most lance-corporals and above have their own single rooms. There are facilities for washing and ironing clothes, sitting and TV rooms. Reasonable deductions from pay are made for accommodation and food (see 'Rates of Pay for Servicewomen' on page 70).

Leave allowance is 30 days a year with pay, and there are extra weekends off. Four free rail warrants are granted each year, and there are other opportunities for cheap travel in Britain and abroad.

If a recruit decides during her first three months in the WRAC that the life is not for her, she can leave without any penalty. Otherwise, recruits are expected to serve for at least three years.

A servicewoman may leave the WRAC on marriage, but this is not compulsory. Where her husband is a serving soldier, the Army will try to post them to the same place if possible. However, women who become pregnant are not allowed to remain in the Army.

WRAC Officers

The sections relating to Army Officers apply to women officers also, except where otherwise stated. See pages 57–64.

Army Scholarship Scheme for Girls

Approximately ten scholarships are awarded to girls in a competition held annually each autumn. The scheme is similar to that for boys (see page 63), but a girl must be over the age of 16 and under 17 years on 1 July, and must have at least one more academic year to complete at school prior to sitting her A-level or equivalent examinations. Applications should be made in the same way as for boys. For full information, see the booklet *Army Scholarship Scheme for Girls* (CP(A)207).

Queen Alexandra's Royal Army Nursing Corps

Queen Alexandra's Royal Army Nursing Corps (QARANC) is a part of the Army Medical Services, along with the RAMC and RADC. Applicants should apply in the first instance to their nearest Army Careers Information Office, and the recruitment procedure follows that for the WRAC except that selection is at the QARANC Selection Centre, QARANC Training Centre, Royal Pavilion, Farnborough Road, Aldershot. All recruits to QARANC complete their eight weeks' basic training at the training centre before moving elsewhere to start their professional or employment training. QARANC employments are as follows:

Student Nurse. (Age limits: 17 years and 10 months to 33 years.) All candidates for Student Nurse training are selected by the Student Nurse Selection Board after personal interview, and by the Personnel Selection Officer at QARANC Training Centre. Training is for three years and leads to the Registered General Nurse (RGN) qualification. A minimum of five GCSE/O levels (or equivalent) at suitable grades are required, and must include English, a science subject and two other academic subjects (preferably including mathematics). Applicants must also achieve a certain standard in the Army Entrance Test. Initial engagement is for four years.

Ward Stewardess. (Age limits: 17 to 33 years.) Works as a member of the ward team in military hospitals under the direction of the ward Sister, relieving nursing staff of non-nursing duties. These include making beds, serving meals, maintaining ward stocks of linen, etc. Initial engagement is for three years.

Clerk RAMC. (Age limits: 17½ to 33 years.) Carries out a variety of clerical duties required by the Army Medical Services. Previous typing experience useful. May be employed in a military hospital providing clerical support in, for example, outpatients and medical records. The preferred qualification is a GCSE/O-level pass or equivalent in English. Initial engagement is for three years.

Dental Clerk Assistant. (Age limits: 17½ to 33 years.) Trained and employed by the RADC. Assists dental surgeon by looking after instruments and preparing materials used in dentistry. Also carries out a variety of associated clerical duties. Assistants may be selected for advanced training, leading to the Certificate of Proficiency in Dental Hygiene. They then qualify as *Dental Hygienists*. Preferred qualifications are two GCSE/O-level passes (or equivalent) in English and a science subject, preferably human biology or biology. Initial engagement is for three years.

Direct Entry for Qualified Enrolled Nurses (General)

(Age limits: under 33 years.) The QARANC has a great deal to offer the qualified EN(G). There are opportunities for further post-enrolment courses and limited vacancies for the shortened course leading to the Registered General Nurse (RGN) qualification. Initial engagement is for three years.

Other QARANC Opportunities

There are limited vacancies for applicants wishing to train as radiographers, laboratory and pharmacy technicians, as well as for qualified physiotherapists. For information about these vacancies, women should contact their nearest Army Careers Information Office.

Rates of Pay for Servicewomen (as at 1 April 1989)

These are the weekly gross rates for servicewomen committed to serve for less than six years (unless otherwise stated).

Private 17 but under 17½	£85.54
Private 17½ and over	£113.12
Private Class III	£125.58
Private Class II	£140.56
Private Class I	£152.53
Lance-Corporal Class III	£152.53
Lance-Corporal Class II	£164.71
Lance-Corporal Class I	£177.45
Corporal Class II with over 6 years' service	£193.13
Corporal Class I with over 6 years' service	£207.20

Examples of QARANC Pay

Private EN (G)	£152.53
Student Nurse Class III	£146.23
Dental Clerk Assistant Class III	£125.58

QARANC and WRAC Officers' Salaries (as at 1 April 1989)

Rank	On appointment	Rising to
University Cadetships (4)	£5,946	£8,198
University Bursary (5)	£1,200	
Short Service Limited Commission	£7,180	£7,672
Officer Cadet	£6,720	
Second Lieutenant (2)	£9,585	
Lieutenant	£12,596	£13,928
Captain	£16,038	£18,641
Major	£20,217	£24,210
Lieutenant Colonel	£27,795	£30,733

Chapter 4
The Royal Air Force

The Royal Air Force exists to maintain a force of military aircraft ready for action at all times. The number of people who actually fly in these aircraft is comparatively small, and consists of the pilot and navigator, air engineer, air electronics operator, and air loadmaster. (The latter trade is open to both men and women.)

The majority of RAF personnel are therefore employed in enabling the aircrews to do their job. When one considers what this requires, it becomes clear why so few are so dependent upon so many. To begin with, airfields and accommodation have to be guarded and kept serviceable; personnel have to be fed and equipped; stores have to be ordered and accounted for; transport has to be provided; and records have to be kept. There must be efficient communications between each RAF station and the Ministry of Defence, as well as between other stations and operational aircraft. In addition, a wide range of mechanical and electronic equipment and weaponry has to be maintained and serviced; aircraft need to be serviced and repaired; fuel for aircraft and motor transport has to be brought in, stored and distributed. Men and women have to be trained. Medical and dental treatment is needed. Personal problems and other welfare matters relating not only to RAF personnel but also to their families have to be sorted out sympathetically. And discipline always has to be maintained, so that each station works as an efficient unit of the whole RAF.

This chapter describes in some detail the work and training of various categories of RAF personnel. It deals first of all with aircrew, both officers and sergeant aircrew, because they are, so to speak, the 'sharp end' of the RAF, the head of the comet. The tail of the comet – officers and other ranks – will be dealt with in that order.

As mentioned in Chapter 1, the RAF is a highly integrated Service. Women officers of the WRAF work alongside male members of the Service, so this chapter will not distinguish between men and women, except to point out those jobs in which women (and in one or two cases, men) are not employed. It will conclude with a brief note on

Princess Mary's Royal Air Force Nursing Service (PMRAFNS), which recruits both male and female nurses.

Joining the RAF

The RAF has set up a number of Careers Information Offices throughout the country (see list with addresses and telephone numbers on page 108). If you are interested in a career in the RAF, the WRAF or PMRAFNS, you should get in touch with your nearest office, and preferably call in. The staff are all experienced airmen or airwomen ready to answer your queries and give you appropriate booklets. They may be able to show you a video illustrating life in the RAF, the training facilities it offers, the range of occupations you might enter, and so on. Whether you wish to become an apprentice technician, a fighter pilot or a nurse in an RAF hospital, you should make your first enquiries at an RAF Careers Information Office. If you are still at school, you will be able to seek advice from your schools liaison officer, and if you are at a university or polytechnic, you should contact the university liaison officer.

Nationality
All candidates for entry into the RAF must satisfy the following conditions with regard to nationality: they and both their parents must be Commonwealth citizens or citizens of the Republic of Ireland since birth, or must have been born in a country which at the time was a part of the Commonwealth or the Republic of Ireland. In exceptional circumstances, these requirements may be waived by the Secretary of State for Defence. All candidates should normally have lived in the United Kingdom for at least five years prior to their application.

How to Join
If you have finally decided you would like to apply for an RAF career, you should talk this over with the NCO at the RAF Careers Information Office, who will discuss with you the kind of work you would like to do, your standard of education, and your various interests. He or she will, if you are still interested, arrange for you to make a longer visit to the office, during which you will take an aptitude test and have a preliminary medical examination. If these show that you are fit enough and you appear suited to the trades you have been discussing, you will then be interviewed by an officer.

Great care is taken over the selection of recruits. No pressure is brought to bear on people making initial enquiries, nor on those who might subsequently make serious applications. The RAF is keen to ensure that no one is enlisted who is not absolutely certain they want to make a career in the Air Force. The recruitment procedure is therefore a fairly slow one, and only when both the RAF and the candidate are certain that enlistment should go ahead is an offer of a place made. It must be borne in mind that there are only a limited number of places available, and competition to obtain them is very keen.

Initial Training

The Initial Officers' Training Course is held at the RAF College, Cranwell, after which officers proceed to professional training at various training stations. Other ranks, whatever trade they might be entering, spend their first six weeks at RAF Swinderby, near Lincoln, where after being kitted out they are initiated into life in the RAF – learning how to recognise the various badges of rank, how to march, salute, and conduct themselves like airmen or airwomen.

Accommodation

During training, airmen and airwomen usually live in dormitory accommodation, but on being posted to an operational station they either have their own rooms or share a room with one or two others. There are facilities for doing washing and ironing, and airwomen usually have hairdressing facilities. For off-duty recreation, there are comfortable clubs with television lounges, snooker and table-tennis tables, and dart-boards. Married servicemen are usually able to obtain a house and garden in a married quarters area, where other RAF families form a friendly and sociable community. Men and women over 18 can apply to live off the station, and this is normally permitted as long as they are able to report for duty on time. They can also apply to have their cars or motor-cycles on the station.

Postings

A first posting to an RAF station will probably last two or three years, but then it will be time to move on. Moving from station to station ensures that personnel practise their skills in a variety of situations, gaining experience as they go. There are opportunities for service outside the United Kingdom. This might be for a few weeks' duration only, to enable personnel to take part in a NATO exercise or engage in equipment trials. But it could last longer for those posted to Germany, Hong Kong, Belize or Gibraltar. There are also a few posts, especially for officers, in foreign countries, where RAF personnel are attached to the embassy staff or act as advisers to other governments.

RANKS	
Royal Air Force	**WRAF**
Marshal of the RAF	
Air Chief Marshal	
Air Marshal	
Air Vice-Marshal	
Air Commodore	Air Commodore
Group Captain	Group Captain
Wing Commander	Wing Commander
Squadron Leader	Squadron Leader
Flight Lieutenant	Flight Lieutenant
Flying Officer	Flying Officer
Pilot Officer	Pilot Officer
Warrant Officer	Warrant Officer
Flight Sergeant	Flight Sergeant
Chief Technician	Chief Technician
Sergeant	Sergeant
Corporal	Corporal
Junior Technician	Junior Technician
Senior Aircraftman — 22|sep oo	Senior Aircraftwoman
Leading Aircraftman (mar oo	Leading Aircraftwoman
Aircraftman 22| Sep 99	Aircraftwoman

The ranks of Chief Technician and Junior Technician are applicable only to certain trades.

Aircrew – Officers

Pilot. There are several different roles for pilots, depending on which squadron they join. They might be employed in air defence, flying fighters such as the two-man Tornado or the single-seat Harrier, or in ground attack. They might have the task of refuelling other aircraft

– a demanding job which enables aircraft to extend their range – or be pilots of the huge Hercules transports carrying supplies or troops. Other tasks include reconnaissance, and patrolling the coastal waters around Britain – a job which is often reported on the national news when there is some off-shore disaster and the RAF is called in to help.

Pilots must first complete their Initial Officer Training, after which they begin a gruelling two-year course. This not only includes training in flying, but also navigation, aerodynamics and advanced military theory. Those trainees who have never flown an aircraft before, or have done less than 30 hours' flying, begin by learning on Chipmunk aircraft at RAF Swinderby. Once they have 30 hours' flying experience, they graduate to Jet Provosts and then to Hawks. By the end of their course, officers will have a clear idea of their future role and will know which type of aircraft they will be flying and what sort of work they will be doing during their first tours of duty.

Navigator. Navigators must also first complete their Initial Officer Training. They then embark on the Air Navigation Course, which comprises 16 months of ground and air instruction. After this they move to the aircraft on which they will be flying when they join their squadron. They too have a clear idea of their future role by the time they have completed the training.

Sergeant Aircrew

Air Engineer. Air engineers are employed on the RAF's larger aircraft, such as Nimrods, Hercules, VC10s, and TriStars. They are responsible for the entire flight performance of these huge multi-engined aircraft, from airframe and engines to the whole range of separate systems. Pilots of these aircraft cannot take off until the air engineer has worked through all the pre-flight checks and cleared the aircraft. There is tremendous responsibility on the air engineer from before the flight until some time after it is over. At take-off, the air engineer handles the throttles and controls the engines' power demands as they change. During the flight, he continually monitors all the aircraft's systems, checks the fuel and its redistribution as it is used up. If anything is shown to be wrong, he must diagnose the fault and attempt to remedy it. Should air-to-air refuelling be needed, the air engineer is in charge of the operation.

Air engineers and other aircrew do not have to join the RAF first and then apply for aircrew training. They should apply for selection while still civilians. Only when they have been selected as aircrew do they need to enlist. They should be between the ages of 17 and 25½, and able to satisfy the educational and medical requirements for aircrew. The selection procedure involves attendance at the Officer and Aircrew Selection Centre for a period of three or four days, when candidates undergo a series of tests and interviews. Those who are selected spend their first six weeks at RAF Swinderby for basic training, and then move on as aircrew cadets to the Aircrew Initial Training Centre at RAF Finningley, near Doncaster. This initial training lasts seven strenuous weeks, at the end of which successful cadets are promoted to acting sergeant. Air engineers and air electronics operators remain at Finningley for another year. Air loadmasters stay there for about three months, during which time they receive some training at an RAF Hospital.

Air Electronics Operator. Air Electronics Operators work in teams, and of necessity have to specialise in certain jobs. They are normally employed on maritime patrol work, flying in Nimrods or Shackletons – large aircraft which are fitted with all sorts of advanced electronic equipment requiring about seven AEOps to handle them. These aircraft are used for locating, identifying and tracking surface ships and submarines. They exercise surveillance over oil and gas rigs and are often called upon to search for missing boats or bring ashore survivors from wrecks or burning ships. Their AEOps specialise therefore in the use of radar, sonar, or underwater sensors to detect submarines, but are capable of handling a wide range of equipment such as computers, photographic apparatus, etc. Some AEOps train as *Radar Operator/Winch Operator* on helicopters. They are responsible for controlling the winch when rescued persons – often injured – have to be winched to safety into a helicopter. The training of AEOps follows that of air engineers.

Air Loadmaster. Both RAF and WRAF personnel may apply for selection as air loadmaster. They may be involved in various jobs in a variety of aircraft. In large fixed-wing aircraft, the air loadmaster is responsible for the safety and comfort of passengers, in the same way as a steward or stewardess on a commercial aircraft. He or she is also responsible for seeing that the cargo is properly and quickly loaded and unloaded, also that it is loaded and its weight distributed in a way which does not impair the performance of the aircraft. When paratroops are being dropped, the air loadmaster oversees their leaving the aircraft, and is the link between the crew on the flight-deck and the men engaged in the drop at the rear.

Many air loadmasters work on helicopters on search and rescue operations and act as *Winchmen*. Their duties may include marshalling the aircraft into confined spaces and picking up underslung loads. Training follows that of air engineers and AEOps, but after the Aircrew Initial Training Course, air loadmasters remain at RAF Finningley for only a further three months' training.

Promotion. When sergeant aircrew go operational after the completion of training, they cease to be Acting Sergeants and become actual RAF Sergeants. Promotion thereafter is to Flight Sergeant and then to Master Aircrew. There are opportunities to apply for or be recommended for a commission.

Other Roles and Trades in the RAF. Having dealt with the actual fliers in the RAF, the remainder of this chapter describes all the other personnel whose efforts enable the fliers to do their front-line work. Some of the details which follow are applicable to the officers and airmen covered in the preceding section which dealt with work and training but gave no details about conditions of service, types of commission, pay, and so on.

Officers

The RAF offers commissions to young men and women who not only have the necessary education or expertise, but the potential to apply their intelligence to almost any discipline. The RAF takes into account a candidate's personality, character, commonsense, powers of leadership, and ability to work as a team member. It is looking, above all, for managers and leaders, people with initiative, able to exercise responsibility in situations where lives or valuable equipment may be at risk, and to inspire confidence in their leadership and loyalty from those in subordinate positions.

Two types of commission are open to candidates: permanent or short service. A permanent commission involves service either to the age of 38, or for a period of 16 years in total, whichever is the longer. It is sometimes possible to serve beyond these periods, until the age of 55. On completion of service, an officer is retired on pension with a tax-free grant. A short service commission is normally for three to six years, the duration varying from one branch to another. However, in the case of pilots and navigators, who need a considerable period of training, short service commissions are for 12 years, with the option to retire after six years' productive service. Officers on short service commissions are usually able to change to permanent commissions if they wish to do so.

Eligibility
Education. Some branches require higher educational qualifications than others, but in most the minimum required is five passes at GCSE/GCE O-level (or acceptable equivalent) in subjects which include English and mathematics. However, the RAF prefers candidates to have A levels.

Applications
Candidates should complete a form obtainable from school or university liaison officers or at RAF Careers Information Offices. Staff at these offices will help them complete the form and will also be able to give them further information about their suitability for particular Service careers. They will then attend a preliminary interview at the Careers Information Office, and if they appear to be suitable, they will be invited to attend a selection board at the Officer and Aircrew Selection Centre. This selection procedure takes about three days, but all expenses (travel, board and accommodation) are paid by the RAF. During the first part of the selection procedure, candidates are tested for intelligence, mathematical knowledge, special aptitudes, co-ordination and perception. They are also medically examined and subjected to a comprehensive interview. Only those who are successful in this first part may go on to the second, which consists of a series of individual and group tests.

The whole process of counselling, application and selection takes time. School-leavers should therefore try to apply at the beginning of their final year, and university students at the end of their second year or beginning of their third.

Sponsorships
The RAF offers a variety of sponsorship schemes to young persons intending to make a career in the Service.

Sixth-Form Scholarships
This scheme is open to boys only, and they must be between 15 and

17 years of age on 1 September of their first A-level year. They should satisfy the conditions for entry on nationality grounds (see details on page 72) and have resided in the United Kingdom for five years prior to their application. They must have, or expect to have, five GCSE/ O-level passes, or five SCE passes at Standard Grade C or above (or acceptable equivalents). The passes must include English and mathematics.

Applications should be made between 1 January and 15 June prior to the September in which the scholarship will commence. Forms are available from the RAF schools liaison officer or the RAF Careers Information Office, and are usually completed during the spring term of the school fifth year. Headmasters are subsequently asked to add a confidential report.

Applicants who appear to be suitable are invited to attend a two-and-a-half-day selection board at the Officers and Aircrew Selection Centre, all expenses being paid by the RAF. Here, candidates undergo various aptitude tests, as well as being medically examined and interviewed. They are notified of the results before the end of the year, and successful candidates receive the first term's award for their sixth form course in arrears. However, unsuccessful candidates should *not* consider their chances of subsequently obtaining an RAF commission affected in any way.

Awards under the scholarship scheme amount to £750 a year, paid to the boy's parents or guardians towards the cost of his studies (which he will continue with in the same way as his classmates). The RAF hopes that holders of a scholarship will join an ATC Squadron or CCF RAF Section, and there is an opportunity for those wishing to do so to take up a Flying Scholarship (see below). They will, however, be given an introduction to the role of an RAF officer by attending a two-week course at the RAF's Outdoor Activities Centre at Grantown-on-Spey, Scotland.

Certain branches of the RAF require entrants to hold a degree or other tertiary qualification, in which case scholars may apply for an RAF University Cadetship (see below). If unsuccessful in obtaining a cadetship, they may nevertheless enter university as civilians and apply to join the RAF either after or during their degree course. Scholars who are successful in their A-level examinations but decide not to go to university are guaranteed a place at the RAF College, Cranwell, for Initial Officer Training.

It must be understood that the Sixth-Form Scholarship Scheme is aimed at young men whose firm intention is to make a career in the

RAF. If a scholar abandons his studies or, having completed his sixth-form course, fails to obtain the necessary qualifications, his parents or guardians must be prepared to refund all the money they have received by way of the award.

Flying Scholarships

These scholarships are open only to young men who are between the ages of 16 and 22 when they apply. Applicants must be Commonwealth Citizens or citizens of the Republic of Ireland, and be in full-time education, or a member of the ATC or CCF. They must have educational qualifications similar to those required for applicants for Sixth-Form Scholarships.

Applications from boys at school or sixth-form college should be submitted between 1 June and 31 December for awards in the following year. Applications from students in higher education should be submitted between 1 October and 31 March if they wish to join the course during the following summer vacation. They must keep up to 28 consecutive days free for this. Application forms are available from the Commanding Officers of ATC Squadrons, CCF RAF sections, RAF schools liaison officers, university liaison officers, and local RAF Careers Information Offices.

Candidates are selected from their application forms, and those who are short-listed are invited to attend the Officers and Aircrew Selection Centre to undergo pilot aptitude tests, medical examinations and interviews. Successful candidates receive 30 hours of free flying at a flying club. The training is on light aircraft, and includes ten hours' solo flying, plus instruction in ground subjects. Although the scheme is designed for young men who are keen to embark on an RAF career, they do not have to make a commitment to do so.

The Air Cadet Navigation Training Scheme

This is a very similar scheme to that for Flying Scholarships, except that it is open to both young men and women between the ages of 16 and 22. The conditions for eligibility are the same, except that applicants must have passed the Air Cadets Air Navigation Examination unless they have GCSE in Navigation, and they must belong to an ATC Squadron or CCF RAF Section. Successful candidates are given approximately ten hours of navigation exercise, flying in a training aircraft such as a Chipmunk.

University Cadetships

Holders of a University Cadetship are commissioned and paid as Acting Pilot Officers from the beginning of their first term at university, or, in the case of those who did not apply earlier, from the beginning of the term following their application. In addition to their salaries, cadets have all the costs of their courses (except board and lodging) paid for them. On graduation, they enter full-time RAF training as Pilot Officers. The scheme is open to both men and women.

Applicants must satisfy the nationality and residence conditions. Those expecting to start a cadetship straight from school should be aged 17½, or should be 17½ during their first term. Other candidates must apply in time to be able to complete their studies by the maximum age permitted for entering their chosen branch of the RAF. Pilots must be able to start full-time training by the age of 24; navigators by the age of 26. Engineers should be under 25 when they begin their degree course, and all other branches expect cadets to be under 23. Applicants who are school-leavers will be invited to attend a 14-day University Cadets Introductory Course at the RAF College, Cranwell, during the summer vacation prior to entering university.

Applicants must have five GCSE/O-level passes, or five SCE passes (or acceptable equivalents), to include English and mathematics. They must also expect to obtain a place on a full-time degree course at a UK university, polytechnic or college. Cadetships are awarded for a period of three years (or four years for students at Scottish universities).

During their course, cadets will be enrolled in their University Air Squadron. Those in the General Duties (Flying) branch will receive extensive flying training, and those in ground branches may take a shorter flying course. Cadets undergo annual training of about a week at Christmas and Easter, and a month in the summer. Their academic studies and training are monitored by staff from the RAF College, Cranwell, and also by the commanding officer of the University Air Squadron. On graduation, cadets enter the RAF College, Cranwell, to begin an 18-week Initial Officer Training Course. Should they, through any fault of their own, fail to graduate, they are liable to reimburse the Ministry of Defence with all the expenses entailed by the cadetship.

Cadetships for men are awarded in the following branches:

General Duties (Flying): Pilot and Navigator
General Duties (Ground): Air Traffic Control, Fighter Control
Photographic Interpretation
Engineer
Supply
Administrative: Secretarial, Education, Catering
Security: RAF Regiment, Provost
Medical and Dental

Cadetships for women leading to permanent commissions are available in the Engineer, Education, and Catering branches.

Cadets may follow the degree course of their choice for most of the branches. For *Catering*, however, a degree course in catering studies is essential. In the *Education* branch, specialisation is preferred in mathematics, computer science, physics or engineering, but some other subjects are permissible. Cadetships in Education are normally available to candidates who have completed a minimum of one year at university and include postgraduate teacher training of one year.

Special conditions apply for *Medical and Dental* sponsorships (see below).

Cadets studying *Engineering* on a sandwich degree course need to find an industrial sponsor for the vocational training part or parts of the course. The RAF will not act as such, except for students on the Air Transport Engineering Course at the City University, London, and on the Electronic and Electrical Engineering Course at Salford University. Cadets on these courses will obtain their industrial experience at RAF stations.

These arrangements apply for a full cadetship occupying the duration of a degree course. On completion of this, cadets are appointed to a permanent commission. However, it is possible for a student to apply for a one-, two- or three-term cadetship in his or her final year of studies, leading to a short service five-year commission, or for a General Duties branch 12-year commission with the option to leave after eight. This arrangement stands if students are about to start, or have already started, their final year of study for Part Two of the Engineering Council Examination. Cadets serve as acting pilot officer during this last year and after graduation proceed to Initial Officer Training. Short service commissions are available to women entrants after one-, two- or three-term cadetships during the final year of study in the following branches:

Air Traffic Control   Secretariat
Fighter Control   Catering
Photographic Interpretation   Provost
Engineer   Education
Supply

University Bursaries

Those who wish to enter the RAF on short service commissions and yet wish to avail themselves of the RAF's sponsorship schemes, should apply for a University Bursary which provides an annual tax-free allowance of £900 over and above the LEA grant. Applicants who have opted for a short service commission of only three years will, however, be granted only one year's bursary. The eligibility and application procedures are the same as for University Cadets, but applications will not be entertained from students with less than three terms of study to complete.

A bursary-holder remains a civilian whilst at university, and is under no obligation to join the University Air Squadron. Failure to graduate may result in the bursary having to be refunded.

Bursaries for Technicians

The RAF also offers a Bursary for two years to applicants who have a place on an HNC/HND course in electrical, electronics, micro-electronics, or electronics systems engineering, or are in their final year of a two- or three-year BTEC HNC/HND course in these subjects. The progression from pilot officer to flight lieutenant of entrants by these methods (Qualified Entry) will be somewhat slower than that of university graduates. They may choose either a short service commission (three, five or six years) or apply for a permanent commission.

The availability of short service commissions is outlined below:

General Duties (Flying): Pilot and Navigator
12 years (with option to leave after 8 years)   Men only

General Duties (Ground): Air Traffic Control, Fighter Control
4, 5 or 6 years   Men and women

Photographic Interpretation
4, 5 or 6 years   Men and women

Engineer
3, 5 or 6 years   Men and women

Supply	
4 years	Women only
5 or 6 years	Men and women
Administrative: Secretarial	
4 years	Women only
5 or 6 years	Men and women
Administrative: Education and Catering	
4, 5 or 6 years	Men and women
Security: RAF Regiment	
5 or 6 years	Men only
Security: Provost	
5 or 6 years	Men and women

Royal Military College of Science, Shrivenham

The Royal Military College of Science is situated near the Cranfield Institute of Technology in Wiltshire, and its academic staff is provided by the Institute. The engineering courses at the RMCS are accredited by the Engineering Council and students are prepared for Cranfield degrees. It is therefore an excellent place for would-be RAF entrants to pursue their studies. The B Eng courses in mechanical engineering, electronic engineering systems and information technology are particularly appropriate for entrants to the Engineer Branch, while the B Sc courses in command, control, communication and information systems are suitable for entrants to other branches where the specific degree course is not stipulated. Applications for University Cadetships should be made to the RAF, which, because the RCMS is not in the university entrance (UCCA) system, will itself make the application for entry to the RCMS. Candidates' UCCA applications to other universities will carry on unhindered while application to the RCMS is being considered.

Medical and Dental Sponsorships

The scheme for University Cadetships applies equally to medical and dental students, but there are some special conditions. Medical students must have passed, or be about to pass, their second MB and be engaged in the clinical phase of studies at a UK university teaching hospital or affiliated medical school. Cadetships will only be offered for up to three years' study, so students should not be more than three years away from qualifying. Dental students must be studying at a UK university and in the last two years of their course, as cadetships are only offered for up to two years of study.

Medical students should apply to:
> OC RAF Institute of Community and Occupational Medicine,
> Aylesbury, Bucks HP22 5PG.

Dental students should apply to:
> Ministry of Defence,
> DM3, Room 827,
> First Avenue House,
> High Holborn, London WC1V 6HE.

A cadetship in medical studies leads to a six-year short service commission, which may at a later stage be extended to a permanent commission.

A cadetship in dental studies leads to a five-year short service commission, also with the possibility of later extension to a permanent commission.

Specialisms for Officers

The work and training of aircrew officers – pilot and navigator – have already been described. Mention has also been made of the various specialisms within the different branches of the RAF. The following sections deal with these in greater detail.

General Duties (Ground)

(a) **Air Traffic Control** is similar to the work carried out in civil aviation. On an airfield, the control staff's responsibility includes the direction of aircraft and vehicles on the ground, and flights within a radius of approximately 30 nautical miles. At an air traffic control centre or an area radar unit, the area covered could be up to hundreds of square miles. Military and civil traffic would be directed up to altitudes in excess of 45,000 feet and co-ordinated with air defence operations.

Professional training begins with 19 weeks at the Central Air Traffic Control School at RAF Shawbury, normally followed by two to two and a half years at an airfield at home or overseas. Area radar training is given in a six-and-a-half-week course at Shawbury.

☐ Age limits on entry: Men: 17½ to under 30
Women: 18 to under 30

(b) **Fighter Control** is part of a round-the-clock air defence operation. Controllers need to be able to use advanced computer technology, to manage a team of high-calibre individuals and

85

to concentrate hard for long periods. They have two main functions: *reporting* involves monitoring and reporting on the radar picture of the region; *control* covers the planning of air operations and the guiding of aircraft to contact positions. The use of advanced fighter aircraft, transportable radars and automated facilities have made these functions highly sophisticated.

Fighter controllers will also be part of the mission crew in the new Airborne Early Warning aircraft. They man the Ballistic Missile Early Warning System, which tracks both missiles and satellites, and the Bloodhound Surface-to-Air missile squadrons.

Initial training takes between 12 and 29 weeks, depending on whether an officer is following a reporting or control path. First postings are to a large command and control station in the United Kingdom.

☐ Age limits on entry: Men: 17½ to under 30
　　　　　　　　　　　　Women: 18 to under 30

(c) ***Photographic Interpretation*** is designed to provide an accurate analysis of enemy or potential enemy situations and intentions. Photographic interpreters work from photographs and films obtained by RAF reconnaissance aircraft. They direct a team of skilled NCOs in this work, and using such tools as a stereoscope, they can produce three-dimensional images from film, and provide an analysis of installations and facilities under surveillance.

There is an 18-week period of initial professional training at the Joint School of Photographic Interpretation. At a later date, it is possible for officers to work with the Joint Air Reconnaissance Intelligence Centre. Postings are either in the UK or to overseas intelligence centres, mainly in West Germany.

☐ Age limits on entry: Men: 17½ to under 30
　　　　　　　　　　　　Women: 18 to under 30

(d) ***Engineers***. There are two streams within the Engineer Branch: *Communication/Electronics Engineers* and *Aerosystems Engineers*. Officers in either branch have to combine a management role with that of practical engineer, for they may have to oversee a staff of up to 50 (and sometimes more) highly skilled tradesmen and women.

Communications/Electronics Engineers work with some of the world's most sophisticated hardware, software and radar systems. They are also involved in the planning, operation and maintenance of revolutionary battle-management systems.

Aerosystems Engineers work on the aircraft's systems – the computer-driven navigation and in-flight defence systems as well as the weapons' selection and aiming and air-to-ground communication systems. They organise continuous repair operations for a whole squadron and ensure that morale and technical standards are kept high. In short, their job is to keep a squadron's aircraft operational, which can also include keeping its motor transport operational too.

Professional training in both streams begins with a 20-week course at the Department of Specialist Ground Training at RAF Cranwell. This is followed by a first posting lasting about two years. After this, engineer officers return to Cranwell for the second part of their training, with specialist training available at a later date. Some officers return to academic study for a further degree during the course of their careers.

☐ Age limit on entry: Men and women: under 39

(e) *Supply Officers* are responsible for the provision of material to meet the RAF's requirements. They are also responsible for the movement of personnel and cargo by air, road, rail and sea. This is an increasingly complex task, which relies heavily upon automatic data processing. The RAF's automated stock-control system is one of the largest in Europe, with most units linked to a central processor, although the larger flying stations operate separate independent facilities.

Supply Officers handle an immense range of items, from complete aircraft and their armament to guided weapons, explosives, fuel, spare components of all sorts, vehicles, small arms, furniture and clothing. They are responsible for ordering all necessary items, their receipt, storage, control, issue, and eventually for their disposal.

Professional training begins with an 18-week Initial Specialist Training Course at the RAF College, Cranwell, and after a first tour of duty, this is followed by further training in specialisms such as movements, fuels, explosives, or data processing and systems design. Subsequent appointments may involve planning the support of exercises or operations, possibly as part of the NATO staffs in Europe.

☐ Age limits on entry: Men: 17½ to under 30 (exceptionally to 39)
Women: 18 to under 39

87

(f) *Administrative*

(i) **Secretarial Officers** work in a number of different specialisms, all of which contribute to the smooth running of the RAF stations to which they are posted. Some deal with the financial side of a station's administration – preparing the budget, forecasting expenditure, paying personnel and overseeing the computer-based accounts systems; others work as estates officers, looking after the RAF's buildings and married quarters – work which involves liaising with officials from the Property Services Agency; yet other secretarial officers are engaged as personnel officers, advising on careers within the Service, dealing with personal problems, attending Courts Martial, and so on.

Their professional training begins with a four-month course at the Secretarial Training School, RAF Hereford. There they are instructed in personnel management, accountancy, housing management, Service law and the handling of personal problems. After one or two postings to gain experience, officers may receive further instruction in special fields such as training, recruiting, computer programming, systems analysis, and intelligence and cryptography.

☐ Age limits on entry: Men: 17½ to under 30 (exceptionally to 39)
　　　　　　　　　　Women: 18 to under 30 (exceptionally
　　　　　　　to 39)

(ii) **Education and Training Officers** work in three main areas: *training support, teaching in formal training courses,* and in *further education.* They give training support by advising on the implementation and development of training schemes for all RAF personnel. They also advise on how to set up training schemes and oversee the use of specialist equipment used in training. They provide the teaching element and academic component on formal training courses, teaching a wide variety of subjects, and may be employed with the Service Children's Educational Authority or engaged in the training of officer cadets at the RAF College, Cranwell. In further education, they ensure the continuing education of RAF personnel in all fields, and offer further education opportunities to RAF families.

Before their first posting, education officers attend a four-week introductory course at the RAF School of Education and Training Support.

☐ Age limit on entry: Men and women: under 30
　　　　　　　　　　　　(exceptionally to 39)

(iii) *Catering Officers* are responsible for food purchase and accounting, food production and service, bar service and accommodation, and personnel management. They arrange in-flight meals for aircrew, and exercise meals for guards and sentries. They may also have to plan major formal and informal occasions – banquets, balls, cocktail parties, candle-light suppers, discos, and indeed royal visits.

They have six weeks' initial professional training at the RAF School of Catering at Aldershot. Their first postings are usually as deputy catering officers on a large unit with perhaps 200 catering staff (though postings are sometimes to smaller units with some 80 catering staff).

☐ Age limits on entry: Men: 17½ to 39
Women: 18 to 39

(iv) *Physical Education Officers* are concerned with promoting fitness, implementing physical education programmes, and promoting and administering a wide variety of sports. They also provide specialist training in military parachuting, survival techniques and adventurous activities.

They undertake a four-week course at the RAF School of Physical Training at Cosford, followed by a two-week elementary parachute training course at No. 1 Parachute Training School, RAF Brize Norton. They may be employed on operational or training units or at specialised schools.

☐ Age limit on entry: Men and women: under 27
(exceptionally to 39)

(g) *Security*

(i) *The RAF Regiment* only employs male officers. Its primary role is the defence of RAF airfields and installations, and it has two main elements: Light Armoured Squadrons and Short Range Air Defence Squadrons. The first element is designed to provide rapid defence against attack by ground forces. It is therefore equipped with Scorpion light tanks and Spartan armoured personnel carriers. The second element is equipped with the Rapier missile system to provide defence against air attack. Officers of the Regiment are in command of teams of tough, fit men, continually practising their military skills and training in the deployment and use of their equipment. Officers also command teams of instructors who train station personnel in combat and survival skills.

Professional specialist training of 22 weeks is undertaken at the RAF Regiment Depot at Catterick, the RAF Rapier Training Unit, and such Army establishments as the Royal School of Artillery and the Royal Armoured Corps Centre.

☐ Age limit on entry: 17½ to 24

(ii) *Provost Officers* are in command of the various police and security units at home and abroad, and of the independent investigation service in the criminal and counter-intelligence fields. Provost Officers on a front-line station might be in charge of 20 or more RAF police, including dog-handlers. They are responsible for advising the station commander on the implementation of RAF security policy, and for the maintenance of discipline and the prevention and detection of crime.

Provost Officers undergo a nine-week specialist course of provost training at the RAF Police School before being posted, normally to an operational station at home or overseas.

☐ Age limits on entry: Men and women: 17½ to under 30 (exceptionally to 39). Preference given to candidates over 21

(h) *Medical Officers* usually begin their careers on an RAF station in the United Kingdom. They form part of a team which includes medical administrators, nurses, health visitors and midwives, and their job is to provide primary medical care for RAF personnel and their families. They also advise on occupational and community medicine problems, assist in the aero-medical evacuation of patients, and may obtain some flying experience. They will, additionally, practise the role they would play in wartime, and go on exercises as required.

After their initial year, Medical Officers may continue in general practice or may elect to specialise and work in one of the RAF hospitals. They might choose to specialise in aviation medicine or aviation physiology, working at the Institute of Aviation Medicine at Farnborough. There are many opportunities for postgraduate training, leading to higher qualifications and accreditation as a consultant.

Officers are also needed in the *Medical Services Branch*, which provides physiotherapists and administrative and logistical support for the Medical Branch. As well as having some basic medical skills, officers are expected to understand accounting, personnel and supply procedures.

☐ Age limits on entry: Men and women: under 39 if fully
registered, under 38 if a houseman

(i) *Dental Officers* serve in all RAF stations both at home and abroad, and those abroad are responsible for the dental care of service families as well as RAF personnel. Dental Officers have charge of dental centres with their staff of assistants, dental hygienists, etc.

There are opportunities for postgraduate research and for specialising in oral surgery at RAF Hospitals.

☐ Age limit on entry: Men and women: under 33

(j) *Legal.* From time to time there are vacancies for qualified and experienced solicitors and barristers. Their functions are to advise on evidence for courts martial, to conduct prosecutions, advise on the implications of the Air Force Act, and assist on legal questions raised by Boards of Enquiry. They also provide advice to personnel under the RAF Legal Assistance Scheme.

☐ Age limits on entry: Men and women: 26 to 32 (but older candidates are considered)

(k) *Chaplains.* The RAF attempts to provide chaplains on all its stations. They are appointed from the following denominations: Anglican, Church of Scotland, Roman Catholic, and Free Churches (including Baptist, Methodist and United Reform). An Anglican candidate should have served not less than two years in priest's orders, and must have the written recommendation of his bishop. Candidates from other denominations are selected on the recommendation of their ecclesiastical superiors.

☐ Age limits on entry: Men only: 27 to 34 (but older candidates are considered)

Officer Pay Scales (as at March 1989)

The RAF system of pay, allowances and benefits is based on a comprehensive Military Salary structure. The Military Salary is designed to be comparable with civilian equivalents, and pay rates are kept under annual review by the Armed Forces Pay Review Body. There is no difference in pay for single and married officers.

Male Officers (RAF and PMRAFNS)

Direct Entrant
The rates of basic pay given below apply to officers in the following categories:

General Duties (Pilot and Navigator)
General Duties (Ground) ie Air Traffic Control and Fighter Control
Photographic Interpretation
Engineer, Supply, Administration, Legal (*note*: this includes women) and Security Branches
Male officers of PMRAFNS

Rank	Annual Rate	Remarks
Officer Cadet	£6,782	
Acting Pilot Officer	£8,428	The top rate for Acting
after 6 months in rank	£8,621	Pilot Officers will only be given to pilots and navigators
Pilot Officer	£9,662	
Flying Officer	£12,713 rising to £14,056	
Flight Lieutenant	£16,184 rising to £18,812	
Squadron Leader	£20,404 rising to £24,433	
Wing Commander	£28,050 rising to £30,999	

Flying and Flying Instructional Pay
Pilots and navigators will in addition to their basic pay receive Flying Instructional Pay at the rate of £365 per annum until they qualify for Flying Pay. For pilots, this is at the start of advanced pilot training, and for navigators on completion of the Air Navigation School Course. Flying Instructional Pay will only be paid to university cadets for the days on which they fly.

Flying Pay	Annual Rate	Remarks
Initial Rate	£2,584	
Middle Rate	£3,971	Awarded after 4 years on lower rate
Top Rate	£4,661	

Women Officers (RAF and PMRAFNS)

Direct Entrant

The rates of basic pay given below apply to women officers commissioned into the RAF in the following branches and to women officers of the PMRAFNS:

General Duties (Ground) ie Air Traffic Control and
    Fighter Control
Photographic Interpretation
Engineer
Supply
Administration

Rank	Annual Rate
Officer Cadet	£6,720
Acting Pilot Officer	£8,351
Pilot Officer	£9,574
Flying Officer	£12,596 rising to £13,928
Flight Lieutenant	£16,038 rising to £18,641
Squadron Leader	£20,217 rising to £24,210
Wing Commander	£27,795 rising to £30,733

University Sponsorship (Men and Women)

Acting Pilot Officer University Cadet:

	Annual Rate		Remarks
	Men	Women	
1st Year	£5,716	£5,665	The rates shown include
2nd Year	£6,402	£6,344	£2,051 Education Grant
3rd Year	£7,099	£7,034	(366 days)
4th Year	£7,880	£7,807	
(Scottish Universities)			

Allowances (Men and Women)
Men and women may be entitled to allowances for travelling on duty, lodging, and overseas service. Removal expenses and disturbance allowances are also payable to entitled married officers whose jobs involve them in moving house. Allowances are usually tax free.

Charges for Accommodation and Food
Single officers living in an officers' mess pay accommodation charges according to their rank and the grade of accommodation. Charges range from £45.63 to £115.00 *a month* for accommodation and are £18.20 *a week* for food.

Typical charges for married junior officers who occupy fully furnished married quarters are £179.15 *a month* for a three-bedroom house.

Retirement Pay
Officers who enter the RAF on a permanent commission, or those short-service officers who are later selected for a permanent commission, will be entitled to retirement pay when they have completed 16 years' reckonable service over the age of 21. Retirement pay is calculated on the number of years an officer has served in his or her rank. These rates are reviewed annually.

A tax-free grant of three times the annual pension is also paid on retirement.

Other Ranks

RAF Engineering Apprentices
Chief among the personnel needed to support the actual flyers are those who maintain the aircraft and their sophisticated electronic systems. These people form a large team of highly skilled technicians whose job it is not only to service the aircraft currently in use – their engines and equipment – but also to keep abreast of developments in a continually changing world of high technology.

In order to obtain the highly skilled technicians it requires, the RAF offers apprenticeships to suitable young men and trains them in its own establishments. This affords a wonderful opportunity for those who are mechanically and scientifically minded, are physically fit, and have the relevant basic education.

RAF engineering, besides being divided into three basic categories – aircraft, electronic, and general – involves three levels of skill: Mechanic, Technician and Engineering Technician. To become an engineering technician, it is essential to enter through an RAF apprenticeship. Through such an apprenticeship, young men can acquire skills which will afford them an excellent career. At the same time they become part of a great team – indeed, a great community – working and living together, enjoying sporting and other activities, and having the satisfaction of doing an important job.

Qualifications

Applications for apprenticeships should be made between the ages of 16 and 18½, although exceptionally applicants will be considered up to the age of 21. Applicants should have four GCSE/O-level passes (or equivalent), to include mathematics and a science (preferably physics). Boys who have not yet been notified of their examination results can nevertheless apply and be considered.

Those who possess these qualifications, are physically fit, and are genuinely interested in a career as an engineering technician in the RAF should apply in the first instance to any RAF Careers Information Office (a list of which is given on page 108). Here they will be able to discuss the matter with the staff and obtain fuller details. The RAF is very careful to make sure that those who join will fit into the Service, be happy there, and stay to make a career in the RAF. Applicants are given various tests and interviews before they are finally accepted.

The apprenticeship course of training is a tough one, requiring a determined effort and plenty of hard work. The end in view is the award of a Certificate of the Business and Technician Education Council (BTEC), although most apprentices find that the training is so thorough they can go on to obtain the Higher National Certificate.

Having passed the medical examination and other tests, applicants begin their training at RAF Swinderby. This is the training centre for recruits, where everyone joining the RAF has to spend a few weeks. Here, recruits are kitted out and instructed in the basic things they need to know as members of the RAF – how to recognise the various badges of rank, how to salute, how to march in step and perform various drill movements on the parade ground. There are lots of physical training, sports and outdoor exercises, as well as training in the use of small arms. The RAF produces a booklet, *Welcome to RAF Swinderby*, which can be obtained by post.

Specialisation

Once the period of recruit training is over, apprentices are selected to train in particular specialisms. They may train to be either *Aircraft Technicians (Airframe/Propulsion)*, or *Electronic Engineering Technicians*. Those who choose electronic engineering are further subdivided into those training to be *Electronic Engineering Technicians (Flight Systems)* and those training to be *Electronic Engineering Technicians (Air Communications/Air Radar)*.

Aircraft Engineering Technicians (Airframes/Propulsion)

After their recruit training, aircraft technicians proceed to RAF Halton, near Aylesbury. They begin their training learning basic engineering skills, such as the use of hand-tools and precision measuring instruments. They then move on to learn how to interpret engineering drawings and to perform various cutting, shaping and reaming jobs. By the end of their second year, they have learned to dismantle and assemble airframes and propulsion equipment. They will understand corrosion control, and be able to apply their knowledge of hand-tools to the repair of aircraft structures. Then, during the third year, they will learn more advanced aspects of aircraft engineering, culminating in the final exercise at the airfield. RAF Halton is not an operational airfield, but many aircraft which have been withdrawn from active service are brought there for training purposes.

Not all the apprentices' time is spent in the workshops. There is a lot of classroom teaching of such things as the principles of thermodynamics, aerodynamics, mechanics, materials technology and machines. Apprentices are given a thorough knowledge of electrical and electronic principles and control engineering, including the use of microprocessors. There are also lessons in mathematics, English, current affairs and general knowledge.

Classes in both the workshop and classroom are small, and instructors are highly qualified and equipped with the most up-to-date teaching aids. During the course, apprentices spend a short time on a flying station to see experienced technicians at work on operational aircraft, and get an understanding of the job for which they are being trained.

Electronic Engineering Technicians

The Electronic Engineering Technicians' Course takes place at RAF Cosford, a station about 20 minutes' journey from Wolverhampton on the railway line to Shrewsbury. Apprentices spend much more of their time in classroom work than do apprentices at Halton. This is because it is essential for them to have a good grasp of the theoretical side of electronic engineering. They therefore concentrate at the beginning of their course on mathematics, (including trigonometry, calculus and statistical methods), physics, mechanical engineering science, engineering drawing, electrical principles, the theory of flight, and computing and control in an avionics context.

In their final year, apprentices are instructed in the advanced electronics appropriate to the specialised trade they have chosen. Those specialising in Flight Systems concentrate on the electronics associated with flight stability and control, and weapons systems. The second group of apprentices, specialising in Air Communications and Air Radar, are instructed in the principles behind the communications, radar, radio, and navigation systems in modern aircraft. Both groups learn to handle analogue and digital computers. They are also made familiar with various engineering publications governing their work, and are taught to understand the documentation involved in servicing aircraft.

Electronic engineering technician apprentices also spend time in the workshops, initially learning skills such as soldering, measuring, and interpreting workshop drawings. The training becomes progressively more complex and demanding, from making up a simple printed circuit from a circuit diagram to wiring quantities of minute components to a circuit board. During the course, apprentices are able to practise on the various aircraft kept for this purpose at Cosford, and midway through their course they go on detachment to a flying station to observe the work of experienced technicians in their trade and to see the air traffic control and communications areas. There is a small amount of air time in the Cosford syllabus during which apprentices are able to gain a little flying experience.

Life as an Apprentice
The RAF schools at Halton and Cosford train other groups besides apprentices. Apprentices are therefore organised into separate flights, each under the command of a flight lieutenant. Although the flight commander has NCOs to assist him, the apprentices take it in turns to be class leader responsible for marching their colleagues to the various places, such as classrooms, gymnasiums, etc, indicated on the timetable. Apprentices who display the necessary leadership potential may be appointed Apprentice Executives in the rank of Leading Apprentice Technician, with the possibility of progressing

to Corporal Apprentice Technician and Sergeant Apprentice Technician. The latter has the distinction of leading the passing-out parade.

Accommodation at RAF Halton is in rooms shared by three or four apprentices. Similar accommodation will shortly be provided at RAF Cosford, but for the time being, apprentices there live in large communal rooms. Three meals are served daily, and there are facilities to purchase snacks and drinks at the NAAFI club in the evening. Both stations have excellent facilities for sport, snooker and table-tennis, and rooms where airmen can relax and watch television.

The apprentice's year is made up of three terms, divided by holidays, and apprentices get six weeks' paid holiday every year. Most weekends are free, although during the first six months, many are taken up with exercises and other organised activities. After their first term, apprentices may bring a car or motor-cycle to their station. They are also granted four free travel warrants a year, which enable them to travel on leave by rail.

Enlistment

Apprentices normally enlist for 12 years, although nine-year engagements may be available. The engagement begins from the age of 18 (or from the date of enlistment for those who enlist at a later age). On completion of the apprenticeship, airmen are posted to their first station as Junior Technicians. They can expect to be promoted to Corporal within two years, and after three or four years may be considered for promotion to Sergeant. Further progress is to Chief Technician, Flight Sergeant and Warrant Officer. Many apprentices are recommended for commissions and some are sponsored for a university degree course, and commissioned directly in the Engineer Branch.

Engineering Technicians

There are 15 different engineering technician trades in the RAF. They are open to men from the age of 16½ and women from the age of 17. The upper age limit is 39. Applicants need a minimum of two GCSE/O-level passes (or their equivalent). Two of the passes must be in mathematics and a science subject.

The engineering trades fall into four groups:

1. Aircraft Engineering Trade	Training unit
Aircraft Technician Airframe	RAF Halton
Aircraft Technician Electrical	RAF Halton
Aircraft Technician Propulsion	RAF Halton
Aircraft Technician Weapons	RAF Cosford
Electronic Technician Flight Systems	RAF Cosford
Electronic Technician Air Communications	RAF Cosford
Electronic Technician Air Radar	RAF Cosford
Electronic Technician Synthetic Trainer	RAF Locking

2. Ground Electronic Engineering	
Electronic Technician Air Defence	RAF Locking
Electronic Technician Airfields	RAF Locking
Electronic Technician Telecommunications	RAF Locking

3. General Engineering	
General Technician Ground Support Equipment	RAF St Athan
General Technician Workshops	RAF St Athan
General Technician Electrical	RAF St Athan

4. Mechanical Transport	
Mechanical Transport Technician	RAF St Athan

Jobs in Aircraft Engineering

Briefly, the task of aircraft engineering technicians of every specialism is to repair, service and maintain the RAF's aircraft, and make sure they are in a state of readiness.

Aircraft Technicians Airframe are responsible for all parts of an aircraft's structure. This includes hydraulics, flying controls, landing gear, air conditioning and pressurisation, oxygen supply, and anti-icing systems.

Aircraft Technicians Electrical are responsible for an aircraft's electrical generation and distribution system, as well as its general instrumentation. This includes generators and alternators, voltage controllers, electric motors and actuators, and airspeed indicators.

Aircraft Technicians Propulsion are specialists in looking after all types of aircraft engines and their control systems, both piston engines and supersonic jets.

Aircraft Technicians Weapons are responsible for ensuring the efficiency of the striking power of an aircraft. They look after the aircraft's armament – guns, rockets, bombs, torpedoes, depth charges and guided missiles. They also look after ejection seats, small arms, and ground defence weapons.

Electronic Technicians Flight Systems specialise in the display, processing, and automatic control systems that provide the aircrew with information. These systems include autopilots, flight directors and stability aids, air data systems, head-up and head-down displays, gyro-compass, intertial navigation systems, and computers for processing navigation and weapon-aiming information.

Electronic Technicians Air Communications service and maintain an aircraft's communications and associated equipment. This includes both long and short range communications, radio compasses, hyperbolic navigational aids, instrument landing systems and radio altimeters.

Electronic Technicians Air Radar are specialists in an aircraft's radar and photographic systems. These include interception, identification and electronic counter-measures installations, aircraft bombing and search systems, tail warning, marine search and doppler facilities, computers, and reconnaissance and gunsight cameras.

Electronic Technicians Synthetic Trainer are skilled in a very demanding specialism requiring an understanding of the principles of flight, and the techniques used in the simulation of flight conditions. Computerised flight simulations are among the RAF's most complex equipment. These, together with other synthetic trainers – procedure trainers, link trainers, and systems trainers – form the equipment in which these technicians specialise.

Jobs in Ground Electronic Engineering

This branch of engineering involves the maintenance, repair, modification and installation of the communications and radar electronic equipment used on the ground. This includes the equipment for air defence, airfield navigational and landing aids, ground-to-air communications, and telecommunications.

Electronic Technicians Air Defence are responsible for the complex electronic equipment, such as the huge radar arrays displayed on the ground for air defence.

Electronic Technicians Airfields specialise in a wide range of airfield radars, airfield navigational aids, landing aids, and ground-to-air communications equipment.

Electronic Technicians Telecommunications service and maintain various types of telecommunication equipment, including high-power high-frequency transmitters and receivers, satellite communications and line telegraphy, much of it associated with the Defence Communications' Network.

Jobs in General Engineering

Engineers in this group provide the support for the other groups, looking after general equipment and lighting, and performing general engineering tasks.

General Technicians Ground Support Equipment maintain and service a wide range of equipment, such as electrical generating trolleys for aircraft starting and servicing; air-cooling and conditioning trolleys; low pressure-air starting trolleys; hydraulic system servicing rigs; air compressors; aircraft jacking; lifting and haulage equipment; airfield arrester barriers; power supplies; and air-conditioning units.

General Technicians Workshops specialise in various tasks, usually one-off or small batch runs, involving the use of centre lathes; drilling, grinding, and other machine-tools; oxyacetylene, electric or inert-gas welding equipment; and general engineering machinery, plant and processes. They are also skilled in blacksmithing and sheet-metal work.

General Technicians Electrical are specialists in all types of electrical equipment used in the support of aircraft servicing and ground operations; airfield lighting; mechanical transport electrical systems; ground radar power supplies; and some domestic electrical equipment.

Jobs in Mechanical Transport

The range of mechanical transport used by the RAF is vast: it includes motor-cycles, staff cars, RAF Regiment armoured vehicles, vans, motor-coaches, articulated lorries, aircraft refuellers, fire tenders, snowploughs, cranes, fork-lift trucks and winches for balloon and glider operations. To service and maintain this great variety of vehicles and equipment, a large number of highly-skilled *Mechanical Transport Technicians* is required.

Technician Training is given by highly professional instructors, who are able to convey very complicated subjects in a straightforward and understandable way. The RAF runs some of the best engineering courses available anywhere in the country and can produce skilled men and women ready to start work at an operational station within 18 months. Nor does it neglect the need for continued training to keep its technicians up to date with new technology.

On successful completion of their training, technicians earn the rank of Junior Technician, from which they can progress to higher ranks (as described in the section on 'Apprentices' above).

Other Trades

Altogether, the RAF can offer 75 trades for its personnel to choose from. Not all of them, however, are open to new entrants, and some require a certain amount of prior experience and specific qualifications.

Everyone in the RAF has a trade of one type or another, and one of the first decisions to be made when a recruit enters the Service is to determine the trade he or she is to follow. After initial training at RAF Swinderby, new recruits are posted to an RAF station which specialises in training them for their particular trade. The length of the training period depends on the trade, but during that time entrants are taught by highly professional instructors. Like the technicians they will be ready at the end of their training to begin duties at an operational station, confident in their ability to do so. However, this is not the end of study and training: promotion examinations are an important feature of the RAF trade structure, so further study is essential for those who wish to advance their careers and prospects.

The following lists are not comprehensive, but they give an idea of the variety of trades, their respective educational requirements and the minimum age at which they can be entered:

1. Engineering Trades

Details have already been given of the type of work performed by the various categories of Technician and Engineering Technician, all of which need the support and assistance of *mechanics*. Mechanics, both men and women, do not need any prior educational qualifications and may enter at 16½ (men) and 17 (women).

The following engineering mechanic trades are available:

Aircraft Mechanic (Airframe)
Aircraft Mechanic (Propulsion)

Aircraft Mechanic (Weapons)
Aircraft Mechanic (Electrical)
Electronic Mechanic (Air Communications)
Electronic Mechanic (Air Radar)
Electronic Mechanic (Flight Systems)
Electronic Mechanic (Air Defence)
Electronic Mechanic (Airfield)
Electronic Mechanic (Telecommunications)
General Mechanic (Electrical)
General Mechanic (Ground Support Equipment)
General Mechanic (Workshops)
Mechanical Transport Mechanic

2. Medical, Dental and Related Support Trades

There are a number of these trades and they all, with the exception of dental surgery and medical assistants, require men and women with some educational qualifications (precise details of which can be obtained from the RAF Careers Information Office). The minimum age of entry into these trades also varies, as shown in the table below:

Trade	Qualifications	Minimum Age	
		Men	Women
Dental Technician	4 GCSE/O levels or equivalent	16½	17
Dental Hygienist	2 — ” —	17	17
Electrophysiological Technician	5 — ” —	16½	17
Environmental Health Technician	3 — ” —	17½	17½
Laboratory Technician	5 — ” —	16½	17
Operating Theatre Technician	2 — ” —	16½	17
Pharmacy Technician	5 — ” —	16½	17
Radiographer	7 subjects including 2 A level or 9 SCE passes including 4 H grade	21	21
Physiotherapist	Professional		
Dental Surgery Assistant	No qualifications	16½	17
Medical Assistant	No qualifications	16½	17

3. Trades Restricted to Men
None of these trades requires any special educational qualifications:

Trade	Minimum Age
Aerial Erector	16½
Fireman	17½
Movements Operator	16½
RAF Regiment Gunner	17

4. Trades Restricted to Women
None of these trades requires any special educational qualifications:

Trade	Minimum Age
Kennelmaid	17
WRAF Shorthand Typist (Qualified)	17
WRAF Typist (Qualified)	17

5. Trades (Other Than Above) (with entry at 16½ years for men, and 17 years for women)
None of these trades requires any special educational qualifications:

Administrative Clerk
Aerospace Systems Operator
Air Cartographer
Air Photography Processor
Assistant Air Traffic Controller
Catering Clerk
Cook
Data Analyst
Painter and Finisher
Photographic Interpreter
RAF General Duties
Steward/Stewardess
Supplier
Survival Equipment Fitter
Telephonist

6. Trades (Other Than Above) (with higher minimum age of entry)
None of these trades requires any special educational qualifications:

Trade	Age of entry	
	Men	Women
Communications Systems Analyst (Voice)	18	18
Communications Systems Analyst	18	18
Mechanical Transport Driver	17	17
Photographer Ground	18	18
Physical Training Instructor	17½	18½
RAF Administration	18	18
RAF Police	17½	18½

Pay for Ground Trades (as at May 1989)

Airmen
Pay on Entry (per week)

Age	16	16½	17	17½ and over		
				Notice	6 Years Fixed	9 Years Fixed
Engagement	All	All	All	Notice	6 Years Fixed	9 Years Fixed
Gross Basic Pay	£63.70	£71.12	£86.31	£114.71	£116.27	£119.42

Pay When Trained

On successful completion of trade training and on passing the appropriate trade test, the following scales of gross weekly pay apply. Pay rates are in three bands, and each RAF trade is allocated to a particular band. (Fuller information about the band to which individual trades have been allocated may be obtained from any RAF Careers Information Office.)

Rank		Notice	6 Years Fixed	9 Years Fixed
Leading Aircraftman	Band 1	£126.70	£128.80	£131.95
	Band 2	£147.56	£149.66	£152.81
	Band 3	£170.17	£172.27	£175.42
Senior Aircraftman	Band 1	£153.93	£156.03	£159.18
(after satisfactory	Band 2	£174.79	£176.89	£180.04
completion of one	Band 3	£197.40	£199.50	£202.65
year's service)				
Junior Technician	Band 1	£179.06	£181.16	£184.31
	Band 2	£199.92	£202.02	£205.17
	Band 3	£222.53	£224.63	£227.78

Promotion to Corporal or above earns higher pay, according to rank, trade and engagement. In addition to basic rates, increments are paid on completion of 9, 12, 15, 18 and 22 years' service and vary from between £3.85 extra per week for a corporal who has completed 9 years to £14.00 extra per week for a warrant officer who has completed 22 years.

Deductions (applicable to airmen and airwomen)

Accommodation: Single airmen accommodated on RAF stations are charged for standard accommodation at the following weekly rates:

Corporals and below: Under 17½ years of age   £6.37
                       Over 17½ years of age   £8.47

Aircrew: On graduation and confirmation of Sergeant rank £15.75.

Food: For single men accommodated on RAF stations, there is a weekly charge of £18.20.

Statutory Charges
RAF personnel are subject to the statutory charges of income tax and earnings related National Insurance contributions.

Pensions, Terminal and Resettlement Grants
Pensions are payable on retirement after a minimum of 22 years' service (rates depend on rank attained and length of service after the age of 18). Those awarded pensions also qualify for a tax-free grant equal to three times the annual rate of pension.

   Airmen who do not qualify for an immediate pension qualify for a preserved pension and terminal grant payable at age 60, provided they have served a minimum of five years after the age of 18. Airmen who complete at least 12 years from age 18 may also receive a tax-free resettlement grant.

Airwomen

Pay on Entry (*per week*)

Age	Under 17½	17½ and over
Engagements	All	All
Gross Basic Pay	£85.54	£113.12

Pay when trained
On successful completion of trade training and on passing the appropriate trade tests, the following scales of gross weekly pay apply. Pay rates, as with airmen, are in three bands:

Rates of pay For those who have served (from age 18 or date of attestation, if later) for		Less than 6 years	6 years but less than 9	9 years or more
Leading Aircraftwoman	Band 1	£125.58	£127.68	£130.83
	Band 2	£146.23	£148.33	£151.48
	Band 3	£168.63	£170.73	£173.88
Senior Aircraftwoman	Band 1	£152.53	£154.63	£157.78
	Band 2	£173.18	£175.28	£178.43
	Band 3	£195.58	£197.68	£200.83
Junior Technician	Band 1	£177.45	£179.55	£182.70
	Band 2	£198.10	£200.20	£203.35
	Band 3	£220.50	£222.60	£225.75

Promotion to Corporal or above earns higher pay, according to rank, trade, and engagement.

Length of service increments, deductions, and pensions, etc, are similar to those for airmen.

Princess Mary's Royal Air Force Nursing Service (PMRAFNS)

Officers

The Princess Mary's Royal Air Force Nursing Service offers a career in general nursing to male and female Registered General Nurses with 12 months' postgraduate experience and a second professional qualification. Nursing officers work in RAF hospitals and are responsible for the nursing care of RAF personnel and their families. In the United Kingdom, RAF hospitals also look after NHS patients. Although they are comparatively small, they offer no lack of clinical variety, and there are units specialising in renal dialysis, plastic surgery and oncology, among others.

Nursing officers are encouraged to broaden their professional knowledge and experience, and opportunities are available to nurse in one of the RAF hospitals in Cyprus or Germany, or to train in aero-medical nursing, which involves the nursing care of patients in transit by air from overseas.

Enrolled Nurses

Candidates must be under 40 years of age, and hold the EN(G) qualification, and their enrolment must be currently registered with the UKCC in accordance with its regulations. They must also pass the RAF entrance test at a Careers Information Office. Recruit training is given at RAF Swinderby and is followed by a course lasting two weeks and two days at RAF Halton, where comprehensive training is given in first aid and special safety. Entrants start with a three-year fixed engagement, which can be extended. There are also opportunities to apply for an RGN conversion course.

Registered General Nurses

The RAF offers opportunities for Registered General Nurses to enter as Staff Nurses on a nine-year engagement. They start as Junior Technicians and after a year are advanced to Corporal. Two years later they should be promoted Sergeant. They might be eligible at any time to apply for commissioning as RAF officers.

RAF Careers Information Offices

Aberdeen
63 Belmont Street,
Aberdeen AB1 1JS (640251)

Aldergrove
RAF Aldergrove,
Crumlin, Co. Antrim
(Crumlin 22738)

Ayr
20 Wellington Square,
Ayr KA7 1EZ (266364)

Bangor
The Drill Hall,
Glynne Road, Bangor,
Gwynedd, LL57 1AH (362850)

Bedford
8–12 Bronham Road,
Bedford MK40 2QA (54278)

Birmingham
14/16 Holloway Circus,
Birmingham B1 1BY
(021-643 6289

Blackpool
10 Edward Street,
Blackpool,
Lancs FY1 1BA
(21144)

Bournemouth
244 Holdenhurst Road,
Bournemouth,
Dorset BH8 8AS (24085)

Bradford
33 Westgate,
Bradford,
West Yorkshire
BD1 2QT (721797)

Brighton
56 West Street,
Brighton, East Sussex BN1 2RA
(27438)

Bristol
Esso Building,
35/37 Colston Avenue,
Bristol, Avon BS1 4TZ (294051)

Cambridge
90 Regent Street,
Cambridge CB2 1DP (358060)

Canterbury
17 St Peter's Street,
Canterbury, Kent CT1 2BJ
(464132)

Cardiff
109 St Mary Street,
Cardiff, South Glamorgan
CF1 1PZ (27626)

Carlisle
9 The Crescent,
Carlisle, Cumbria CA1 1QW
(23359)

Chatham
3 Dock Road,
Chatham, Kent ME4 4FJ
(Medway 45285)

Coventry
Broadgate House,
Upper Precinct, Coventry,
West Midlands CV1 1NU (25003)

Darlington
148 Northgate,
Darlington,
Co. Durham, DL1 1QT
(461850)

Dundee
171 Overgate,
Dundee, Angus DD1 1QF
(26839)

Edinburgh
21 Hanover Street,
Edinburgh, Midlothian
EH2 2DN (031-225 3114)

Exeter
Fountain House,
Western Way,
Exeter, Devon EX1 2DE
(54204)

Glasgow
Charlotte House,
78 Queen's Street,
Glasgow, Lanarks G1 3DN
(041-221 4852/3)

Gloucester
Lister Buildings,
Station Road,
Gloucester GL1 1HE (24538)

Grimsby
241 Freeman Street,
Grimsby,
South Humberside DN32 8DW
(50350)

Guildford
Steward House,
Sydenham Road,
Guildford, Surrey GU1 3SR
(573511)

Huddersfield
26 Kirkgate,
Huddersfield,
West Yorkshire HD1 1QQ
(25345)

Hull
82/83 Prospect Street,
Hull, North Humberside
HU2 8PE (25903)

Ilford
180 Cranbrook Road,
Ilford, Greater London
IG1 4LB (01-518 1411)

Inverness
3 Bridge Street,
Inverness IV1 1HG (235610)

Ipswich
58 Princes Street,
Ipswich, Suffolk IP1 1RJ
(58157/53989)

Leeds
10 Bond Court,
Leeds, West Yorkshire LS1 2JY
(432914)

Leicester
84 Charles Street,
Leicester LE1 1GH (24940)

Lincoln
19/20 Saltergate,
Lincoln LN2 1DN (30601/2)

Liverpool
53 London Road,
Liverpool,
Merseyside L3 8HY (051-207 0588)

London
Kelvin House,
Cleveland Street,
London W1P 6AU
(01-636 0782)

Luton
18/19 West Side Centre,
off Dunstable Road,
Luton, Beds LU1 1ES (24805)

Manchester
Barnett House,
53 Fountain Street,
Manchester M2 2SL
(061-236 8289)

Middlesborough
69 Borough Road,
Middlesborough,
Cleveland TS1 3AD
(243026/210665)

Newcastle
9 Ridley Place,
Newcastle,
Tyne and Wear NE1 8LP
(2328748/2325708)

Newport
4–5 Kingsway,
Newport,
Gwent NP9 1EX (53873)

Norwich
6 Bridewell Alley, Norwich,
Norfolk NR2 1AH (614616/7)

Nottingham
70 Victoria Centre,
Milton Street,
Nottingham NG1 3QX (476407)

Oldham
70 Union Street,
Oldham,
Greater Manchester OL1 1DJ
(061-624 4961)

Oxford
35 St Giles,
Oxford OX1 3LJ (52661)

Peterborough
23 Hereward Centre,
Peterborough,
Cambridgeshire PE1 1TB
(69669)

Plymouth
69/73 Mayflower Street,
Plymouth, Devon PL1 1QR
(664572)

Portsmouth
11 Arundel Way,
Portsmouth, Hants PO1 4NY
(821938)

Preston
83A Fishergate,
Preston, Lancs PR1 2NJ (54218)

Reading
Liverpool Victoria House,
Cheapside, Reading,
Berks RG1 7AH (590650)

St Helens
7 George Street,
St Helens,
Merseyside WA10 1DA (20571)

Sheffield
1 The Gallery,
Castle Market Buildings,
Exchange Steet,
Sheffield,
South Yorkshire S1 1FZ
(720070/729970)

Shrewsbury
7/8 St Mary's Street,
Shrewsbury,
Shropshire SY1 1EB
(51292/247972)

Southampton
153 High Street,
Southampton,
Hants SO1 0BT (225239)

Southend
524 London Road,
Westcliff-on-Sea,
Southend,
Essex SS0 9HS (345739)

Stoke-on-Trent
36/38 Old Hall Street,
Hanley,
Staffs ST1 3PD (29386/272777)

Sunderland
4 Burdon Road,
Sunderland,
Tyne and Wear SR1 1QB
(5677551)

Swansea
Llanfair Buildings,
17/19 Castle Street,
Swansea,
West Glamorgan SA1 1JF
(55643/54573)

Swindon
18 Milton Road,
Swindon,
Wilts SN1 5JN (21654)

Taunton
35 East Street,
Taunton,
Somerset TA1 3LS
(283708)

Truro
107 Kenwyn Street,
Truro,
Cornwall TR1 3DJ (76445)

Wolverhampton
23 Victoria Street,
Wolverhampton,
West Midlands WV1 3PD
(27595)

Wrexham
21 Rhosddu Road,
Wrexham,
Clwyd LL11 1NF
(266033/266137)

York
4 New Street,
York,
North Yorkshire YO1 2RA
(28264)

Index